To Bobbie – loved cleatting with you – sorry you
don't live here – XX Lilly

Essentially Lilly

Essentially Lilly

A guide to colorful entertaining

Lilly Pulitzer AND Jay Mulvaney

PHOTOGRAPHS BY BEN FINK   ILLUSTRATIONS BY IZAK ZENOU

HarperResource

An Imprint of HarperCollinsPublishers

ESSENTIALLY LILLY: A GUIDE TO COLORFUL ENTERTAINING

Copyright © 2004 by Sugartown Worldwide, Inc.

All rights reserved. Printed in China.

No part of this book may be used or reproduced in any manner whatsoever without written permission

except in the case of brief quotations embodied in critical articles and reviews.

For information, address HarperCollins Publishers Inc., 10 East 53rd Street, New York, NY 10022.

HarperCollins books may be purchased for educational, business, or sales promotional use.

For information, please write: Special Markets Department, HarperCollins Publishers Inc.,

10 East 53rd Street, New York, NY 10022.

First Edition

CONCEIVED AND PRODUCED BY 1919 LLC. New York www.1919.com

DESIGNED AND COPRODUCED BY Vertigo Design NYC www.vertigodesignnyc.com

ILLUSTRATIONS © 2004 by Izak Zenou. Represented by Traffic NYC

PHOTOGRAPHS © 2004 by Ben Fink, except those listed below.

Horst P. Horst/*Vogue* © Condé Nast Publications, Inc., *page vi*
Elizabeth Kuhner, *pages viii, 4 (l, r), 9 (l), 11 (l), 14 (l)*
Bob Davidoff, *pages 2 (r), 14 (r)*
The estate of Howell Conant Jr., *pages 3, 7, 8, 11 (r)*
Slim Aarons/Getty Images, *page 13*
Todd Eberly, *page 15*
Kate Kuhner, *page 16 (l, r)*

"You Are My Sunshine" *page 167* © 1940 by Peer International Corporation.
Copyright Renewed. International Copyright Secured. All rights reserved.

LIBRARY OF CONGRESS CATALOGING-IN-PUBLICATION DATA
Pulitzer, Lilly.
Essentially Lilly : a guide to colorful entertaining / Lilly Pulitzer and Jay Mulvaney ;
photographs by Ben Fink ; illustrations by Izak Zenou.
p. cm.
ISBN 0-06-057749-5
1. Entertaining. 2. Cookery. I. Mulvaney, Jay. II. Title.
TX731.P83 2004
2003056748
642'.4—dc22

04 05 06 07 08 TP 10 9 8 7 6 5 4 3 2

To N.S.W.

A friend may well be reckoned

the masterpiece of nature.

— RALPH WALDO EMERSON

Contents

Barefoot Queen of the Jungle

In the heart of Palm Beach—a town famous for its clipped lawns and manicured hedges—lies a tropical jungle of banyan trees and palms, of ferns, ginger and heliconia. Ripe mangos fall to the ground with a soft thud while flowering gardenias glisten against their dark green leaves. Lush and inviting, this jungle is a world set apart from the grandeur and the gilt that surrounds it on all sides. It's a peaceful oasis, and reigning over it all is a barefoot queen called Lilly.

There is no brass door knocker at the gates of this paradise, just a big monogrammed letter L. It's just as well, too, as any knocker would have rusted in place as sure as the Tin Man's ax. One learns quickly that you don't bother to knock, or, God forbid, ring the bell at Lilly's. Just walk in the door and holler out "Hey Doll" and make your way to the kitchen, or outside to the pool or over to the slat house. There you'll find her, in a hot pink shirt and crisp white slacks, mixing a bowl of food for her menagerie of cats, with a visiting grandson—"I love you Granny" calls out the strapping twenty-year-old as he dives into the pool—and a ringing phone—eleven rings until the machine picks up, enough time to get in from the way back—and something sizzling on the big outdoor grill.

Welcome to the jungle.

Outside Palm Beach Lilly is known as Lilly Pulitzer, creator of a dress that bears her name and a style that effortlessly captures the delectable balance of affluence and ease. But inside that illustrious sliver of sand she is Lilly Rousseau, loved by all, and celebrated not for whom she is but for how she lives—with gusto, generosity and a never-ending sense of fun.

Lilly in her jungle, circa 1966.

Lilly's spirit is big enough to embrace both of these personas—the public Lilly Pulitzer, whose clothes have dressed three generations of women up and down the east coast, and the private Lilly Rousseau, who, having made Palm Beach her permanent home fifty years ago, rarely strays far from her tropical Eden. She is very happy indeed with her role as matriarch, mother, grandmother and friend. While she moves from one persona to the other with the same ease in which one slips into her signature "Lilly" dress, it's obvious to those who know her which one she truly embraces.

Lilly loves people—and she loves to entertain them—and does it better than just about anyone else. To paraphrase Oscar Wilde: "Lilly gives her talent to her work, but her genius to her life."

Her parties are legendary. People love them almost as much as they love her. Why? It's not about the food, although it is "you-lead-a-good-life-and-the-angels-take-you-to-paradise-and-this-is-what-they-serve-you-to-eat" good. It's not about the decorations: whimsical pink-and-orange balloon bouquets atop Chinese export ceramic peacocks festooned with Kenny Jay Lane rock crystal and gold bead necklaces. It's not about an "exclusive" guest list; on the contrary, her parties are *inclusive,* including everyone from the grand dames of society to visiting firemen to the friends who used to work for her.

Lilly's parties are about her "peeps"—her people, a collection of friends as eclectic as her décor and as vivid as the colors that adorn her clothes. "I love to be surrounded by people," Lilly says.

And so she is. Many don't wait to be invited, they just show up. "Sometimes I'll have sixty people for dinner."

For Lilly, there's as much fun to be had in the hours leading up to her parties, when preparations are in full swing. Good hostess that she is, she sets you up with a task—punching out bread rounds, chopping bacon and spreading peanut butter to make one of her favorite "crispy crits"—the minute you walk in the door. "I will demonstrate *once* the way I want this done," she'll say, "and then leave you on your own."

The hallmark of Lilly's entertaining style is elegance, although not in the way one might normally describe the word. Lilly's elegance doesn't come from fancy china or heirloom silver (though she has plenty of both). Her elegance comes from her innate desire to see people enjoy themselves in her home, to have a delicious meal, to feel welcomed and cherished. And do they ever.

LEFT TO RIGHT:
Lilly with her sister Flo and their children, circa 1964. Lilly and Peter Pulitzer, 1966.

She loves to entertain, and has forever—in the 1960s *Town and Country* astutely proclaimed that "Hostessing is a favored pastime of the people-collecting Pulitzer." (They got that right.) There are few things Lilly enjoys more then having people come to her house for a party.

Lilly is the consummate hostess. Yet, when asked her secret for successful entertaining, she scoffs, "Secret? There's no secret … just have fun. Don't worry about every last little thing. Somehow it always works out."

That could easily be her philosophy about life as well. And what a life she has—Lilly Pulitzer is the real "Palm Beach Story."

🌴 🌴 🌴

Lillian Lee McKim Pulitzer Rousseau is an American original in every sense of the word. Born into a New York world of rarified privilege, with servants to tie one's shoes and private railroad cars in which to travel from one city to another, Lilly lives by the credo of the true aristocrat—to "treat a duke like a dustman and a dustman like a duke."

"As a child, I was always being told *not* to be so familiar with the staff. But I couldn't help it," she says with a twinkle, "they were all my buddies."

Though "to the manor born" Lilly has always been a rebel. After a socially impeccable schooling at Chapin, Miss Porter's and a short tenure at Finch, she was restless. She wanted to taste more of what life offered than the very restrictive choices she was born and bred to make. "*THAT* kind of life wasn't for me," Lilly tartly comments, "I wanted to *do* something." As her schoolmates were making their debuts, Lilly was riding a donkey through the hills of Kentucky, working for the Frontier Nurses Service. When her friends were waltzing in their wedding splendor, she was toiling as a nurse's aide at the Veterans Hospital in the Bronx.

🌴

When it came time for her to marry, there were no orange blossoms and no canopy at St. James's Church. "I eloped when I was very young, around twenty or twenty-one, and we moved to Palm Beach, where I've lived ever since."

Lilly and her first husband, Peter Pulitzer, turned heads when they came to Palm Beach in the 1950s. They were, in the memory of her friend Sunny Bippus, "the most gorgeous couple imaginable." Then they made the unusual decision to live year-round in what was traditionally a winter resort community. "Palm Beach was a different place in those days. Oh, in the summer it was dead. D-E-A-D. They would take down the streetlamps and put sand down on the roads. Maybe two or three stores would stay open all year-round. It was a ghost town."

Lilly wasn't concerned. "I didn't set out to be unusual or 'different,'" she says. "I just wanted to do things my way."

Like her parties. The Pulitzers were known for giving the best parties in town. Everybody came to their big clapboard house on Lake Worth. Theirs was an affluent life, but it was famously unstuffy.

"We put in a big kitchen," Lilly says, "and we practically lived there. Our dinner parties were very casual, with everyone pitching in to chop and slice, everyone dancing and singing." Making your kitchen the center of home entertaining is commonplace nowadays, but back then it was unheard of. And *all* Palm Beach flocked to the Pulitzers. Guests would include Gerald and Florence Van der Kamp (he ran Versailles for the French government) and Nelson Doubleday (sister Flo's husband, he owned the New York Mets as well as the publishing house that bears his name). Nellie would tend bar and Gerry would don one of Lilly's wigs and everyone would take the empty champagne bottles, fill them with water, and slick down the kitchen's tile floor for dancing. It was relaxed, casual, fun. Good times.

But all was not as it seemed. "To be honest, when we got married, I was not the most mature kid on the block," Lilly says, adding, "I couldn't do a lot for myself; I was namby-pamby. People always made decisions for me.

"So I went out to the New York Hospital in Westchester. In the old days we called it Bloomingdale's because it was where all of us 'fashionable' ladies went to have our breakdowns. The doctor there said, 'There's nothing wrong with you, you just need something to *do*.' I followed his advice and came out of the hospital a lot stronger, and I haven't stopped since."

As was her wont, when Lilly arrived at the crossroads, she chose the unconventional path. In 1950s society, men worked and women stayed at home. Lilly, ever true to herself, became an entrepreneur.

Mogul in motion. Lilly and Peter, 1963.

"My husband had orange groves down at Fort Pierce. He flew down there every morning and came back with bags of oranges. I would drive around to the back of all the big houses and sell the fruit out of my station wagon. I tell you, I knew every cook, every butler, every maid in Palm Beach. I had a wonderful time. I then graduated to selling gift boxes of fruit. I booked so much business that Peter told me that he couldn't afford to *give* me the oranges anymore; I'd have to start *buying* them. So I opened a tiny shop selling oranges on the Via Mizner."

Out of that tiny shop Lilly would launch her forty-year reign as, "a major force in Prep resort wear," lauded by everyone from the *New York Times* to the *Preppie Handbook*.

LEFT TO RIGHT:
Lilly's shop in the
Via Mizner, 1962.
Lilly on the
beach, 1963.
The Via Mizner
today.

The Via Mizner is a series of interconnected courtyards and covered walkways tucked behind the big shops on Worth Avenue. A creation of the famed Palm Beach architect Addison Mizner, it is Mediterranean in spirit and filled with red-tile roofs, climbing bougainvillea vines, little shops and mossy green fountains.

Visiting the Via Mizner with Lilly is like following the Pied Piper of pink and green. "She's one of the greats," says Dominick Dunne (whose late wife, Lenny, was a longtime friend from Miss Porter's). "She is a joyous lady with more friends than anyone I know. Everybody loves Lilly," he says, and it's true. People stop what they're doing, come over to her and are heartily embraced and engaged in conversation. Lilly knows everyone, really cares about them and is both unstinting with her praise and frank with her advice. "She has a whole different brand of generosity" is how her son-in-law Kevin McCluskey sums up her spirit.

Lilly walks over to a very small shop whose bowed front wall is a checkerboard of glass panes, and points with bemused pride to the site of her first store. "There was a little juice and fruit bar in the back right there. I would slice the oranges and squeeze the fruit to make the juice. My friends would stop in and we would just talk and laugh and have fun. The twist had just hit Palm Beach, so the Lilly shop was where it was all happening. But, boy, was it messy. At the end of the day I was covered in pulp and dribbles of orange juice. I had to do something.

"I used to have this wonderful old Swiss lady make shifts for me. I found this bright, *bright* fabric, the same colors as the fruit, so that the splashes and mess wouldn't *show*. People would say, 'Oh, they're great. Why don't you have them in the shop?' So I went down to Woolworth's, got some fabric and had twelve dresses made for me, and I just hung them haphazardly around the store.

"This was the early sixties. The Kennedys were down here," she says of that unique moment in Palm Beach history; "Jack had just been elected president. The eyes of the whole world were on Palm Beach.

Jackie wore one of my dresses—it was made from kitchen curtain material—and people went crazy. They took off like zingo. Everybody loved them, and I went into the dress business."

As we walk through the Via Mizner to its neighbor, the Via Parigi, Lilly keeps pointing to the different locations where her "fun little" business kept growing: "Lilly Kids was right here, Lilly Tennis was over there, and all this—men's, boutique, swim and golf," she says, sweeping her arm to indicate four or five different shops, "was Lilly central."

"Lilly central" turned out to be more than an array of shift dresses in flamboyant patterns and wild colors. Lilly became the uniform of the gentry "at ease," becoming as much a talisman for a particular segment of society as navy blazers and twin sets with a strand of pearls.

The "Lilly"—a dress best described as "a cross between a chemise and mumu"—has been a staple in the wardrobes of casually chic women for three generations. The very real sense of happiness that comes from donning a "Lilly" comes from the attitude with which Lilly embraces life. It's hard to feel logy when you're swathed in raspberry pink and tangy orange.

"It was hot-weather dressing, very resort, and colorful in a time when color just exploded," says Lilly's friend Susanna Cutts. "The 'Lilly' was liberating to wear. It skimmed the body, it was sleeveless, collarless. All you needed were your Luigi sandals and your own real jewelry and you could go anywhere." And anywhere means *anywhere*—devoted fans have been known to leave firm instructions that they must be buried wearing their favorite Lilly.

"And why not?" asks Lilly. "You know they're headed somewhere fun if they're wearing one!"

🌴 🌴 🌴

Lilly's business expanded throughout the 1960s. "I grew up a lot too. I got divorced and later married this divine Cuban man. I built a new house where we continued to entertain and have fun."

But by the mid-1980s, Lilly had had her fill: "It worked for twenty-three years, but it wasn't going to work forever. People change, people move on and, to be frank, I didn't have the smarts for it—I couldn't run a business in the eighties like I did in the sixties. I was spoiled and so used to doing whatever I wanted when I wanted. How great was that! My theory used to be, who says you can't do it!"

It might have been time for Lilly to move on but her customers felt abandoned. Times may have changed but the ladies loved their "Lillys." They treasured the vintage dresses, skirts, even the pull-on pants made from 1970s industrial-grade polyester ("Oh, those pants were great," says Lilly, warbling, "You're the top, you're the Polly Pull On"). They clamored for more. When the Lilly Pulitzer fashion line

Palm Beach ladies in their Lillys, spring 1964.

🌴

was revived in the 1990s it was enthusiastically welcomed as an antidote to a monotone (and to Lilly's many fans, monotonous) world. And now Lilly Pulitzer fashion is back, as carefree and colorful as ever.

"That's good," says Lilly. "It's good because these clothes make people happy. You feel *happy* wearing a bright color. It makes you smile. And who doesn't want to smile a little bit more these days?"

❋ ❋ ❋

The Lilly Pulitzer clothes have always been more than just something to wear; they stand for a way of living and entertaining and having good times. And there's an interesting parallel between Lilly Pulitzer clothing and Lilly Pulitzer's parties. Both are comfortable, colorful and relaxing. Both appear to be casual

and effortless. Yet both are based on solid foundations—the "Lillys" with their full linings and dressmaker details and the parties with their firm grounding in the rules of etiquette. Lilly's secret in both arenas is to know the rules but to be comfortable enough to break them every now and then.

Tips on entertaining and decorating and the like are offered with more than a little reluctance. Not so much because they are state secrets, but because in all facets of her life, Lilly applauds individuality. Having always marched to her own drumbeat, she wants everyone else to do the same. No "do-it-my-way" maven, she.

When pressed again for hints on successful entertaining, Lilly offers two witty tips: "Never cook clever" and "Never practice on guests. You don't want your guests to be victims."

LEFT TO RIGHT:
Queen of the jungle, 1990.
Lilly's son Peter Pulitzer with wife, Amy, and daughters Emma and Charlotte.

Lilly with her
daughters and
their families.

ON THE LEFT:
Liza with her partner
Philip Roome, and
grandsons Bobby
and Chris Leidy.

ON THE RIGHT:
Minnie and Kevin
McCluskey, grand-
children Rodman
Leas, Jack McCluskey
and Lilly Leas, 2003.

The way Lilly entertains values serendipitous fun over fastidious planning; it's about going with the flow and not being tied down to schedules. It's about laughing when the poached salmon slips off the platter and falls to the floor just as your friends arrive for dinner (follow Julia Child's example and put it right back on that platter). It's about waking up in the morning in anticipation of the day's new adventure.

An important thing to know about Lilly is that she doesn't have a "lifestyle," she has a life, and there's a real distinction between the two. You don't "have" to do anything in a specific way to thrive in Lilly's world, except be true to yourself. Dress it up, dress it down, but that's the real deal.

Today, Lilly lives surrounded by laughter and family and friends and color. A small "d" democrat, Lilly's world is populated with members of her extended family (daughters Liza Pulitzer and Minnie McCluskey, son Peter, several grandkids, her sister plus a platoon of steps, in-laws, exes and so forth), life-long friends (school chums from Chapin and Miss Porter's) and the people whose work makes life easy in Palm Beach (the checkout clerks at Publix, the gardeners who tame her lush tropical jungle and the snappy waitresses at Hamburger Heaven, the local joint that Lilly and her friends call "our club").

Lilly's life is active, with little time for nostalgia or looking back. But when you can get her to talk about the old days, she does so with a smile. "Now I look back at my life and think this is not so bad. This cute gypsy girl and that cute guy and then that other cute guy—it was crazy."

While the crazy days of squeezing oranges in a tiny storefront may be little more than a distant and pleasant memory, Lilly's outlook is as colorful as ever and her life as vibrant. She, like the clothes that bear not only her name but also the stamp of her effervescent personality, is about today. Spending time with Lilly, whether it's walking through the Via Mizner with her or leafing through these pages filled with stories of her favorite parties and tempting recipes, makes you think of her favorite song from *La Cage aux Folles*:

"The best of times is now. . . . "

How wonderful yellow is. It stands for the sun.

—VINCENT VAN GOGH

Mellow Yellow Mornings

MINNIE'S

Red sky at night, sailors' delight.

SUNRISE SAIL

Red sky at morn, sailors be warned!

—AN OLD SAILOR'S DITTY

Peter used to have a beautiful sailboat," Lilly says of her early married life. "We used to go over to the Bahamas and watch the sun come up. You're closer to nature when you sail. You have to work with everything, and not against it, the way you do with a powerboat. In sailing you get the essence of working with nature, working with the water and the wind."

"My kids love to sail as well," Lilly adds. "My son Peter goes off to Scotland and France sailing for three or four weeks every summer. And my daughter Minnie and her husband Kevin—they're true sailors."

"The ocean is part of my soul," confesses Lilly's daughter Minnie McCluskey. "I would never live away from the water."

Sailing offers a feast for the senses—the sting of the salt spray on your face, the sound of the lines and the sails and the wind rushing by, the warmth of the sun, the vision of a limitless horizon. Why not enjoy a sail by going out at daybreak?

"Going out early in the morning is fantastic," says Lilly. "It's absolutely beautiful. The seas won't be so rough, there will be just a little bit of a breeze and in the long days of summer it will be a little bit cooler. It is *the* most unique way to entertain friends," she adds. "Get them out of bed early; drag them to the boat if necessary. They'll bless you for it once you're out on the water."

To go out on a sunrise sail, plan to leave the dock by 6:30 or 7:00. You don't really need to be on the water as the very first ray of sunlight breaks over the horizon, but there's something magical about being out at first light. There's often a little haze over the water and the light

what to serve

LEMON-BLUEBERRY MUFFINS

CROISSANTS

JALAPEÑO BLOODY MARYS

AVOID ANYTHING GREASY, LIKE PEANUTS OR CHIPS, THAT MIGHT STAIN THE BOAT'S TEAK DECKING.

is soft and golden. The water, still calm itself, offers some quiet, peaceful moments as you witness the world waking up.

Whether it's a small daysailer or a forty-eight-foot catamaran, whether it's your boat or one you rent for the day, sailing is by its nature an informal way to entertain. Bring a couple of friends along, stop by a local bakery for some basic nibbles and some strong coffee and make sure you're wearing the proper footwear (like the Beatles album, your shoes must have a rubber soul) and you're set to go. An hour or two, first thing in the morning, makes for an invigorating start to the day.

Why sail rather than use a motorboat? Well, that's the secret joy. "The pleasure I get from sailing," explains Lilly, "is that I don't really care about where I'm going. It's the experience of getting there that

makes it so totally enjoyable. In a powerboat it's the 'getting there' that counts. It's just a mode of transport. In a sailboat, when the breeze is just right, well, it sounds corny, but you're more in harmony with nature. It's fantastic."

There's also the satisfaction of persevering. Sailing takes a lot of work to master. And it can be hard; "the pleasure comes when the pain stops" is a saying familiar to anyone who has learned to sail. But the rewards are well worth the effort. Once the skills of sailing have been mastered, you are rewarded with the ability to harmonize with nature.

"On a morning sail your friends can see the most incredible things," recounts Minnie with enthusiasm. "We have porpoises down here still, and they swim along next to your boat. You see hawksbill turtles and leopard rays, which are like other rays only spotted like leopards. It's so incredible."

"I've been on boats forever," she says. "My dad used to have this great boat, called the *Serendripity*, because it always leaked. We'd go out and see the most amazing things."

What's where on a boat...

The word **posh** will help your left hand know what your right is doing onboard a boat of any size, from a humble dingy to the QE3. An acronym for *Port Over, Starboard Home,* posh was at one time a reminder to book accommodations on the left side of the ship while steaming across the Atlantic, and the right side for the return voyage. This would have your cabin facing north, out of the glaring sun in those pre–air conditioned days of luxury travel.

And if all that leaves you adrift, just remember that port and left have the same number of letters. *Fore* (forward) and **aft** (the back of the bus) are a snap in comparison.

...and what's what onboard

It's not a kitchen, it's a **galley**
It's not a bathroom, it's a **head**
They aren't ropes, they're **lines**
It's not a bedroom, it's a **cabin**
It's not a bed, it's a **berth**
There are no windows, there are **portholes**
They're not the staff, they're the **crew**
And, it's not a ship, it's a **boat** (How to tell the difference? You can put a boat on a ship but you can't put a ship on a boat.)

Sailors find that their senses are particularly heightened on an early morning sail. The sea, the salt, the strong smell of coffee all merge into an intoxicating aroma that is specific to the morning. Be sure to dress in layers; as the day progresses you'll be able to stay comfortable by peeling down.

"What I really love about a morning sail," says Minnie with a laugh, "is that it's not so crowded with other boats early in the day. No one can reach you, there are no cell phones. We love to bring some good friends along, drop anchor and scuba dive and swim."

"In fact," her husband Kevin adds, "it was during just such a morning sail, when we were dating, that it hit me that we had to get married."

Romance on the high seas—is there a better endorsement for an early morning sail?

Lemon-blueberry muffins

MAKES 12

½ cup (1 stick) unsalted butter

1½ cups sugar

3 large eggs

1½ cups all-purpose flour

½ teaspoon baking soda

½ teaspoon baking powder

½ teaspoon salt

¼ cup freshly squeezed lemon juice

1 tablespoon finely minced lemon zest

½ cup sour cream

2 cups fresh blueberries

Coarse sugar

1 Preheat oven to 375 degrees. Lightly butter standard-size muffin tin. Using electric mixer, cream butter and 1½ cups sugar. Add eggs one at a time, beating between additions.

2 Whisk flour, baking soda, baking powder, and salt in medium bowl to blend. Add dry ingredients to egg mixture in three additions, beating well between additions. Add lemon juice and zest and beat to combine. Gently fold in sour cream, then blueberries.

3 Spoon batter into prepared muffin tin, filling each about ¾ full (bake any leftover batter in custard cups or ramekins). Sprinkle tops of muffins with coarse or additional regular sugar, using about ¼ teaspoon of sugar for each. Bake muffins until tester inserted into center comes out clean and tops of muffins are golden, about 35 minutes. Cool slightly; turn out of muffin tin and serve warm or at room temperature.

Jalapeño bloody marys

This spicy and fresh-tasting take on the classic brunch cocktail makes it ideal for warm-weather entertaining. Garnish with skewered vodka-soaked grape tomatoes and lime wedges dipped in paprika.

6 TO 8 SERVINGS

5 cups tomato juice

1 jalapeño, seeded, coarsely chopped

1 cup vodka

⅓ cup freshly squeezed lime juice

1 tablespoon prepared horseradish

1 tablespoon Worcestershire sauce

1 teaspoon hot pepper sauce

¼ teaspoon coarsely ground black pepper

1 In large blender, combine tomato juice and jalapeño; blend until pureed.

2 Pour tomato mixture into large pitcher. Add vodka, lime juice, horseradish, Worcestershire sauce, hot pepper sauce and ground black pepper; stir until combined well. Cover and refrigerate until cold, at least 3 hours.

3 Fill glasses with ice. Pour Bloody Marys over ice. Serve, passing additional hot pepper sauce and vodka.

SUNNY YELLOW

Why, sometimes I've believed as many as

BREAKFAST

six impossible things before breakfast.

IN BED

—ALICE'S ADVENTURES
IN WONDERLAND

*E*ntertaining comes in many guises—sometimes it's a sit-down dinner for twenty-four and sometimes it's just breakfast in bed. "I *love* the whole idea of breakfast in bed," says Lilly. "Imagine starting your day with such pampered luxury. If you have houseguests, make their stay a little bit more special by bringing up a breakfast tray. Or, if you're busy with kids or career (or both), what could be more sumptuous than to treat yourself to a bit of a lie-in, an extra hour or two in the morning to just cozy down and do whatever tickles your fancy?"

If you save your best china, crystal and silver for special occasions, make breakfast in bed an occasion with a capital O. Raid the pantry and the silver vault for granny's sterling, Great-aunt Flo's hollow

stem champagne glasses and those Rosenthal Bokhara dishes that were such an extravagance that you could only afford two place settings when you first got married. Use all those wedding gifts that spend most of their lives on display but are rarely used.

If you can swing it, the best way to enjoy a breakfast in bed is to have someone else prepare it and serve it to you. If it's the cook's day off (or if every day is the cook's day off), consider having your breakfast catered. For a very special occasion, find a private chef through a

the menu

BAKED BANANA FRENCH TOAST
WITH GINGER-MAPLE SYRUP

BACON

TROPICAL FRUIT BELLINIS

CAFÉ CON LECHE

culinary school or a catering service. Or ask one of your friends who's a great cook to come in and prepare it. If you're skilled in the kitchen, consider offering this to your houseguests or as a gift to a good friend.

Today is the day to completely satiate your cravings and have the kind of sinfully rich breakfast that would have made it absolutely impossible for Scarlett O'Hara to lace up her stays. Take your favorite breakfast and rev it into high gear. If you like French toast, how about French toast stuffed with bananas and smothered in a ginger-maple sauce? Are Bellinis your beverage of choice? Infuse them with your favorite tropical fruits. Coffee? Add heated milk for a café con leche.

For your—or your guests'—aural pleasure, listen to some favorite CDs. Continue to indulge yourselves by watching a DVD or video. Pick one of your favorite movies or choose something that you've always wanted to see but never got around to—make it a morning matinee.

Scrumptious breakfasts seem to run in Lilly's family. "Can I tell you what my husband does for me," says Minnie. "Kevin does the most incredible things for special occasions like our anniversary or

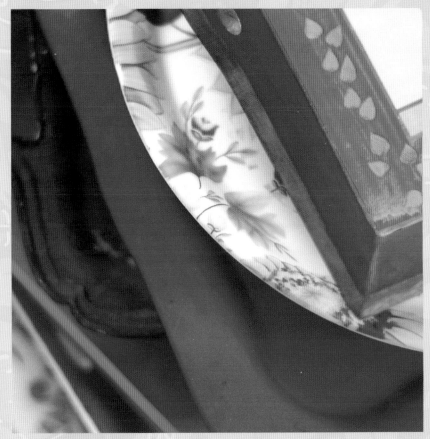

Mother's Day or my birthday. He'll make me breakfast, there will be vases of flowers, these wonderful linens, and he'll even make sure the kids are occupied. Once he even filled the bed with rose petals. How special is that?"

The best marmalades

If you can find it, the very best marmalade is Cora's Sweet and Sour, made with Cora Evan's family recipe and from oranges from her own orange grove in Winter Park, Florida. It's the combination of Temple oranges with one sour orange that makes it zing. Or is it the fact that the eighty-eight-year-old Cora still climbs up her own citrus trees to handpick the choicest fruit?

If you don't know Cora, try Elsenham's Handmade Fine Cut Tangerine Marmalade, Carmine's Tangerine Marmalade or Palmalito's Orange Marmalade.

(Available at specialty food stores and gourmet markets.)

Breakfast with a view

If you want to combine breakfast in bed with a fabulous getaway, try one of these small hotels famous for pampering their guests.

Auberge du Soleil. Rutherford, CA—Perched on a hillside overlooking the vine-covered Napa Valley.

Little Palm Island. Little Torch Key, FL—A tropical paradise. Thurston and Lovie Howell never had it so good!

The Point. Saranac Lake, NY—A former Rockefeller lodge on the shores of a pristine Adirondack lake.

The Ranch at Steamboat Springs. Steamboat Springs, CO—A ski resort overlooking the Yampa Valley.

Wheatleigh. Lenox, MA—The most luxurious small hotel in America, nestled in the Berkshire hills.

Baked banana french toast with ginger-maple syrup

Put this dish together the night before; the next morning it will be ready to serve after only half an hour of baking. Lightly toasting the challah makes stuffing it easier; skip the toasting step if using a day-old loaf.

2 SERVINGS

1 to 1½-inch-thick slices challah (from 1-pound loaf)

1 large banana, cut on diagonal into ½-inch-thick slices

2 large eggs

1 cup whole milk

¼ cup whipping cream

1 teaspoon vanilla extract

½ cup pure maple syrup

1 tablespoon minced candied ginger

¼ cup slivered almonds, toasted

Powdered sugar

Shaved peaches and melon (optional)

1 Butter small baking dish (9x9x2-inch square cake pan or similar). Lightly toast challah. Using small sharp knife, cut slit in bottom edge of each slice of bread to form pocket; insert 3 to 4 slices of banana in each. Place stuffed bread in single layer in prepared dish.

2 Whisk eggs in medium bowl to blend. Add milk, cream and vanilla and whisk to blend well. Pour mixture over bread slices in dish, basting to coat well. Cover tightly with plastic wrap and refrigerate overnight.

3 Combine syrup and ginger in small saucepan; cover and refrigerate overnight.

4 In the morning, preheat oven to 375 degrees. Uncover French toast and bake until puffed and just beginning to brown on top, about 25 minutes. Meanwhile, heat syrup-ginger mixture over low heat.

5 Sprinkle baked French toast with toasted almonds and powdered sugar. Top with shaved peaches and melon, if desired, and serve with warm syrup.

Tropical fruit bellinis

For an alcohol-free tropical fruit sparkler, omit the sugar and substitute either sparkling apple cider or ginger ale for the sparkling wine. The fruit puree can be prepared one day ahead; cover and refrigerate until ready to use, then combine with sparkling wine and serve.

MAKES 4 DRINKS

½ mango, peeled, coarsely chopped

½ peach, peeled, coarsely chopped

¼ cup guava nectar

¼ cup apricot nectar

2 tablespoons sugar

1 750-ml bottle Prosecco or other sparkling white wine

1 Combine first 5 ingredients in blender; blend until fruit is pureed. Measure ¼ cup fruit mixture into each wineglass. Add ½ cup sparkling wine to each glass, stirring gently to combine. Serve immediately.

AN EARLY
Patsy may have gone walking after midnight,

RISER'S
I go first thing in the morning.

RAMBLE

—LILLY

O ur first house was on Lake Worth, right next to the Lake Trail—a pathway that goes up the whole inland side of the island," Lilly says. "I would be out there every morning, first with the babies in the strollers and later on bikes. My kids grew up on the Lake Trail. When they were older, I would go out walking, just by myself—listening to some great upbeat music—or with some friends. I loved it. You could look at people's houses and peer in their windows. If you got out early enough you could even see Monsieur and Madame having breakfast on the porch. I'd wave and say hi.

"I used to listen to one of Jane Fonda's tapes. It really was the best," she remembers. "You would put on your headphones and you couldn't stop your feet from walking out the front door. I'd skip down the driveway. I was always looking at other people's houses and mentally cutting hedges, or painting shutters or replanting window boxes." How far would she go? "Oh," she says with a laugh, "you'd just walk until you fell in a swoon in the gutter."

If you don't live in Palm Beach, chances are still good that you do live near *someplace* outdoors! So, go outside and just walk. if you like the beach, that's terrific. If you live in the city, go to a park. If you don't live near a park, walk around your local high school track. "Just get up, get out, get going," says Lilly.

Walk this way

Yes, it's putting one foot in front of the other and going forward, but with a little extra effort, your morning walk will provide you with a whole slew of benefits. Read *Jay Walking: The Ultimate Fitness Journey* by Jay Ciniglio.

Scavenger hunting

As you walk along the beach, keep your eyes open for interesting shells, stones and pieces of beach glass. Take the beach glass to your jeweler and have it set in sterling silver to make charms, earrings or cufflinks. Put the shells and pebbles into a large crystal bowl and use as a centerpiece on your dining table.

First thing in the morning—those quiet hours before the world revs up, before the cell phones start ringing and before the emails start piling up—is the best time for a walk. The weather is more pleasant, the air is more fresh and there's a special camaraderie to be found between early risers, a sort of secret society that understands the benefits of getting a good start early on in the day. Plus, if there's good gossip, you'll be the first to hear it!

"Go out with a couple of girlfriends," recommends Lilly's friend the Palm Beach artist Binny Jolly. "You can visit, make your plans for the day, rehash all the news from yesterday. I like to go early in the morning because it's cooler."

What to listen to if you're going solo

If it's hard to find the time to sit down and read, books on tape are a wonderful alternative, and often they're read by the authors themselves.

Autobiographies are the best.

Try *Barbara Bush: A Memoir*, the funny and surprisingly tart remembrances of one of the two women in American history to be both the wife and mother of a president, or *The Kid Stays in the Picture*, movie producer Robert Evans' whisky-voiced tale of his wild adventures in Hollywood. Or consider *A Walk in the Woods: Rediscovering America on the Appalachian Trail* by Bill Bryson. (And if you live anywhere between Maine and Georgia, you can walk along the trail.)

If you're feeling social, go out with a friend or two for some easy conversation. Bring the dogs and take a romp on the beach. "Get that feeling of sand squishing between your toes," as Lilly puts it. If you're feeling more solitary, go out to be reflective and "recharge your battery." Either way you get some wonderful exercise.

You can walk at a clip, amble along or take a leisurely stroll. Search the beach for pretty shells—"see what

the tide washes up," says Lilly. "There's coral rock, tritons, conch shells or pieces of the old beach glass, smooth and colorful as precious gemstones."

You can also witness nature at its most glorious. "In Palm Beach, May to October is nesting season for sea turtles," says Binny. "You can see the nests as you walk along the beach and you can watch as the little baby turtles make their way to the sea. It's fantastic." The big nests are marked by stakes so no harm comes to the eggs.

You get so much out of a morning walk and the benefits are not only physical: "My mind gets really clear," says Lilly. "Things don't bother me so much by the time I reach the end of my walk."

THE "G & T" BRUNCH

Lilly girls never wear tennis whites.

They only wear white underwear.

—LILLY

olf and tennis are the two great games of country club life. A proficiency in either is a calling card. "The first thing people ask you is if you play tennis or golf," says Lilly. "If you know how to play, you're invited everywhere."

Entertaining and sports go hand in hand and run the gamut from tailgating parties outside football stadiums to dinner dances at the country club. After a morning on the links or the court, why not relax over a leisurely brunch—at the club, as a picnic al fresco or back at home.

Lilly lives in the part of Palm Beach that the locals refer to as being "between the clubs"—that is, south of the Everglades (for golf) and north of the Bath and Tennis (famous for their Dusty Millers—vanilla ice cream smothered in hot fudge sauce, then dusted with malt). The Everglades and the "B&T" are the two old guard clubs in town— no wet bathing suits in the dining rooms and golf skirts of a decorous length. There are many different clubs catering to varied interests—the Sailfish for the young family crowd, the Beach Club,

the Breakers, the Palm Beach Club and others. But in a class all by itself is Mar-a-Lago.

Once the home of cereal heiress Marjorie Merriweather Post, her husband, E.F. Hutton and their daughter, Nedenia (the actress Dina Merrill), Mar-a-Lago was turned into a private club by its new owner, Donald Trump. It is unique in that it offers its members and their guests the experience of visiting a grand Palm Beach house much as it was in its heyday. Its lavishness, literally, has to be seen to be believed. Lilly says, "It reminds one of the compliment playwright Moss Hart once said about his partner George S. Kaufman's country home: 'It's what God would have done if He had had the money.'"

Now, of course, one of Lilly's primary tenets is that money and entertaining don't necessarily go hand in hand. Nice as it is to have, you don't need a well-padded bank account to entertain with style and imagination. If you belong to a country club, that's great. Meet friends there, or bring your out-of-town guests with you for brunch.

If you don't belong to a club, have a picnic brunch after tennis or golf. Liven it up with your own plates and linens—use colorful sheets as extra large picnic blankets or tablecloths. Make it a colorful, festive brunch. You could plan a brunch at home that coincides with the finals at Wimbledon or one of the PGA championships.

Any way you choose, all you need to do is sit back, enjoy brunch and enter the debate over which is the better game: golf or tennis.

an off-menu menu

ORANGE ICED TEA

POTATO AND ONION FRITTATA WITH AVOCADO AND SALSA

ROASTED ASPARAGUS WITH LEMON AND TOASTED NUTS

DULCE DE LECHE CRÊPES WITH FRESH FRUIT SKEWERS

"Golf," says Lilly, but that might just be out of sibling loyalty. "Our Flo, my sister Flo, she's our golfer. She has won the Everglades championship for the last three years."

"It's hard to say," muses Liza Pulitzer. "Tennis is less time consuming, but golf is more intimate . . . they say you can learn more about people from playing a round of golf with them than you can working next to them for a year."

Lilly's friend Colleen Orrico counters, "Oh, no question. Tennis is definitely a better game than golf because it's actually exercise and, besides, the outfits are so much cuter."

Golf courses for "the girls"

Lilly's great friend Ann Downey, the decorator and former amateur golf champion, says these courses are tops!

Amelia Island Plantation, Amelia Island, FL
The Boulders, Carefree, AZ
The Broadmoor, Broadmoor, CO
The Greenbrier, White Sulphur Springs, WV
Pebble Beach, Spy Glass,
Pebble Beach, CA

Pinehurst #2, Pinehurst, NC
Pine Needles Lodge & Golf Club,
Southern Pines, NC
Reynolds Plantation, Greensboro, GA
Seminole, North Palm Beach, FL
Shinnecock, Southampton, NY

Tennis anyone?

Every year sees a quartet of grand slam tennis events. Each receives extensive television coverage, but if you're a tennis fanatic, why not plan a vacation around attending one or more (or even all!) of them?

US Open. New York in September—chic visitors choose the Mark Hotel on the Upper East Side.

Wimbledon. London in July—the Halcyon just off Holland Park is a little gem of a hotel.

Australian Open. January down under—a hidden treasure of Sydney is the Harbour Rocks Hotel.

Roland Garros (the French Open). Paris in June— for a grand slam event, stay in the grande dame of Paris hotels, the George V.

Orange iced tea

Stir together equal parts of your favorite iced tea with fresh squeezed orange juice. Ice if you like and add a big slice of orange!

Potato and onion frittata with avocado and salsa

For a fancier version, skip the cheese and crown each wedge with sour cream whisked with fresh dill or chives, and a teaspoon of caviar.

6 SERVINGS

2 Yukon Gold potatoes, peeled, cut into ¼ inch cubes (about 2 cups)

12 large eggs

1 teaspoon salt

½ teaspoon ground black pepper

2 tablespoons olive oil

1 medium Spanish onion, peeled, chopped

1 cup chopped green onions (from 1 bunch)

1 cup grated pepper jack cheese

1 large avocado, peeled, sliced

Sour cream

Fresh salsa

1 Bring medium pot of salted water to boil. Add potatoes and cook until tender, about 8 minutes. Drain well; rinse with cold water.

2 Whisk eggs, salt and pepper in large bowl to blend well.

3 Heat 2 tablespoons olive oil in heavy large skillet over medium high heat. Add onion and sauté until translucent and tender, about 6 minutes. Add green onions and sauté until just wilted, about 1 minute. Stir in cooked potatoes.

4 Pour egg mixture over potato-and-onion mixture in skillet; reduce heat to medium low, cover and cook until eggs are set around edges of pan, about 12 minutes.

5 Preheat broiler. Uncover skillet and sprinkle frittata with grated cheese; broil, watching carefully, until cheese melts and browns in spots and frittata is set in center, about 4 minutes. Remove from oven and let stand 2 minutes. Cut into wedges and transfer to plates. Top each wedge of frittata with ⅙ of avocado slices. Serve, passing sour cream and salsa separately.

Roasted asparagus with lemon and toasted nuts

2 pounds fresh asparagus

¼ cup olive oil

1 tablespoon fresh lemon juice

½ cup chopped toasted macadamia nuts or toasted pine nuts

salt and pepper

1 Preheat oven to 500 degrees. Bend ends of asparagus, snapping where they break naturally. Discard tough ends. Spread asparagus out in single layer on large rimmed baking sheet. Whisk olive oil and lemon juice in small bowl. Brush asparagus with mixture, turning to coat all sides. Sprinkle asparagus generously with salt and freshly ground black pepper.

2 Roast asparagus until crisp-tender, bright green and just beginning to brown in spots, about 7 minutes. Sprinkle toasted nuts over asparagus and serve.

Dulce de leche crêpes with fresh fruit skewers

Start preparing the crêpe batter one day ahead to save time on the day of the party. Dulce de leche, a rich milk caramel sauce, is available at most specialty food stores.

6 SERVINGS

2 cups whole milk

¾ cup all-purpose flour

4 large eggs

5 tablespoons butter, melted

1½ tablespoons sugar

½ teaspoon salt

½ fresh pineapple, peeled, cored, cut into 1-inch pieces

12 small strawberries

1 mango, peeled, cut into 1-inch pieces

1 kiwi, peeled, coarsely chopped

6 10-inch bamboo skewers

1¼ cups dulce de leche or other prepared caramel sauce

1 teaspoon vanilla extract

2 tablespoons additional butter

1 Combine milk, flour, eggs, butter, sugar and salt in blender; blend 1 minute, scraping down sides. Pour batter into medium bowl; cover and chill at least 2 hours or overnight. Rewhisk before using.

2 Assemble fruit skewers: alternate pineapple, strawberries, mango and kiwi pieces on skewers. Place in glass baking dish; cover and chill until ready to serve.

3 In heavy small saucepan, stir dulce de leche and vanilla extract over low heat. Meanwhile, melt additional butter in another heavy small saucepan. Brush 8- to 9-inch nonstick skillet with butter. Heat over medium high heat. Pour ¼ cup crêpe batter into skillet, tilting skillet to cover bottom. Cook until crêpe is golden brown on bottom, about 1 minute. Using spatula, gently flip crêpe and cook on other side until golden brown, about 1 minute. Transfer to plate.

4 Drizzle 1 teaspoon warm dulce de leche over crêpe; fold in half and then in quarters, and transfer crêpe to baking dish. Repeat with additional butter as needed, batter and dulce de leche, making a total of 12 to 16 crêpes. Rewarm crêpes in 350-degree oven if necessary.

5 Place two filled crêpes on each plate. Place one fruit skewer on each plate. Drizzle plate, crêpes and fruit with some of remaining warm dulce de leche, and serve immediately.

TREASURE

It's just somebody else's trash,

HUNTING

but I love it!

—LIZA PULITZER

*g*rowing up chez Lilly means a from-the-cradle exposure to big-E eclectic taste. Both of the houses that Lilly has called home in Palm Beach—the turn-of-the-century clapboard house on Lake Worth and the rambling Mizner-inspired palazzo that she designed for her jungle paradise—are examples of a determinedly mix-it-up style that blends stateliness with a marvelous vibrancy that makes her home inviting and comfortable for her guests.

In Lilly's world less isn't more—more is more. You find layer upon layer of the most amazing objects. It's a visual feast of botanical prints, ceramic elephants, Asian screens and beaded chandeliers, painted French country furniture, modern glass tables, whirligigs, wicker and Wedgwood. "I think my mother had a terrific eye" is how Lilly explains it. "She had a very eclectic taste in furniture and loved mixing up strange and wonderful stuff. I had always been around it; it had always been in me."

Super swap meets

ABROAD:

Bermondsey, London.
Bring a flashlight and arrive at 5:30 AM on Fridays.

Marché Biron, Porte de Clignancourt, Paris.
Saturdays to Mondays.

Porta Portese Market, Rome.
Sunday mornings for a real Roman experience.

Togo Flea Market, Tokyo.
First and fourth Sundays of each month.

Casa Barata, Tangier.
It's a daily market and perhaps your only chance to utter the phrase "take me to the Kasbah!"

AT HOME:

Brimfield Show, Brimfield, MA.
Three times a year.

Rose Bowl Swap Meet, Pasadena, CA.
Second Sunday of each month.

South Florida Fairgrounds, West Palm Beach, FL.
First weekend of every month.

Southampton Classic, Southampton, NY.
Twice a summer.

Twenty-sixth Street Arcades, New York City.
Andy Warhol's favorite haunt, open every Sunday year-round.

Lilly inherited some of her "strange and wonderful stuff" from her mother and acquired even more, including a large array of paintings from contemporary artists—"the dead ones don't have to eat."

Living with a combination of wonderful things whetted her daughter Liza's appetite for unique objects. Introduced to the sport of what she describes as "hunting for treasures" by a friend, she is now an avowed spelunker. What's the thrill of flea market shopping? "Well," Liza says, "it's the search that's really exciting. You just never know when you're going to find that piece that makes you go, 'Oh my God, perfect!'"

"It's also the greatest way to entertain friends," Liza adds. "Either your friends who share the collecting bug or friends from out of town who want a real taste of the local scene."

Depending on where you live, these tag sales—variously called flea markets, swap meets and jumble sales—are the place to find that exceptional piece to add just the right accent to a room. Be it Limoges demitasse cups, porcupine quill boxes or Dansk cookware, you can find just about anything at a flea market. With just a little bit of skill and practice, you can take home a one-of-a-kind beautiful object for a one-of-a-kind bargain price.

Liza's craze for the hunt started in London. "A girlfriend and I used to go down to the Bermondsey market first thing in the morning, way before the sun came up, and poke around in the back of all the dealers' trucks.

"You eat that peasant breakfast, fried bread with egg and sausage and brown sauce, and then you're all set to go, spending the morning wiping the dust off with your hands to get a better look and finding some great stuff."

Back in the States, Liza goes flea market shopping almost every weekend. Hopping into a big empty car with a like-minded girlfriend or two, she sets off to one of the many markets near Palm Beach.

Yes, there is eBay, and even the big auction houses have on-line auctions and sales, which makes it more convenient if you are looking for a specific item (a replacement piece of your silver or china, or some vintage Lilly Pulitzer clothes). But there is nothing as wonderful as finding that diamond in the rough, that Lalique vase that someone's been using as a toothbrush holder or that tole tray that's been hidden in the barn for decades. Go off with some friends and turn the morning into a social event. Wear bright colors so you can spot each other through the hoards. And set a few ground rules if your tastes are similar—you don't want to end up like Lucy and Ethel wrangling over the same embroidered tea cloth! Know your friends' tastes and be on the lookout for things they might like (or might like as gifts come Christmas).

Flea markets can be as large as the massive Brimfield Show that takes place in a meadow the size of three football fields or as small as a garage sale in a little beach bungalow. The fun is that you never know where something really wonderful is going to pop up. It's such a truism that "one man's trash is another man's treasure." After a while, you learn to trust your instinct. If it's a tag sale at someone's home, do a slow drive-by and see if their taste in general is something you find simpatico→be it Island Tropical, Early American or Danish Modern. If something strikes your eye, get out, walk around, take a closer look and strike up a conversation with the seller.

The same approach works when you go to a big destination sale like Brimfield or the Rose Bowl swap meet, which attracts movie stars like Diane Keaton and Meg Ryan in search of everything from mission furniture to antique Rolex watches. See what catches your eye, take heed of your instincts and don't be too shy to ask questions.

Both professional dealers and homeowners weeding out clutter will respond to an enthusiastic and sincere appreciation of an object that they acquired because they just loved it and had to have it (at one point, anyway).

Another thing that sellers respond to, and even expect of you, is to engage in a little bit of dickering back and forth over cost. You can expect to pay at least ten percent less than the first asking price. And sometimes, especially at the end of the day, when the thought of packing up a huge tea service or oil painting seems daunting, you may be able to negotiate quite a significant bargain.

For those who were brought up to believe that talk of money and bargaining over price is distasteful, a tactful approach is best: "I love this sterling baby's rattle. If I were to take the linen tea cloth too, would you be able to offer a better price?" A pleasant and gracious demeanor works wonders. There are the horror stories of people demanding a sharp discount—"I want a better price for this," say, thirty-dollar lamp with a silk shade that alone originally cost almost five times as much.

"OK, you want a better price," the put-upon dealer may respond. "It's now sixty dollars."

Or consider the classic story of the arrogant customer who held up a ten-dollar ceramic vase and said to its owner: "Will you take a dollar for this?"

The seller took the vase, looked at it for a moment, dropped it on the ground, where it shattered into a dozen pieces, and responded, "Now I will." A more gentle approach will work wonders!

Once you get your trinket home—and many of the larger markets are allied to companies who can arrange for larger pieces to be shipped if need be—set it in pride of place and just absorb it into your life.

"The most killer thing I ever found in a flea market," Liza recalls, "is an amazing giant tortoiseshell that's so white I think it must be albino. It's almost three feet tall and hangs in a place of honor in my house.

"That's just what's so fun about shopping in a flea market. You spend a great day with some friends and then you go home with your twenty-dollar treasure."

A trio of tips

1. Start early—the early bird catches the worm AND the Meissen dessert plates.
2. Bring plenty of small bills. It's easier to bargain if you don't crack out a hundred-dollar bill.
3. Look up high and down low for the stuff that others don't see. One savvy shopper found a Georg Jensen flatware service for twelve crammed in a shoe box on a bottom shelf, which she happily purchased for fifteen dollars!

What to take with you

1. Water, especially if you're going to an outdoor market.
2. A power bar or energy bar. If you don't want to stop for lunch, this will keep your enthusiasm from flagging.
3. A brightly colored sweater or shirt so your friends can easily spot you when they come across that Kosta Boda platter you've been searching for.
4. A tape measure and an accurate set of dimensions—for those large pieces of furniture or garden sculptures.
5. Your friends. Make it a social scavenger hunt!

Best buys

1. Check local newspapers for estate sales, often you'll find "instant heirlooms"—silver with a lovely patina or mossy garden pots.
2. Opposites attract—lower prices! Rural areas are destinations for "Ye olde country" seekers. Modern things sell for a song.
3. Incompletes sets—seven dinner plates or five place settings—are considered less valuable. Grab them and serve dinner for four!

Wear pink and make the boys wink!

—LILLY

Think Pink Afternoons

BLUSHING

Going to the Chapel of Love?

BRIDESMAIDS'

Who needs to go anywhere?

LUNCHEON

It's right out back.

— LILLY

O ut in the middle of Lilly's jungle is the slat house. Originally built for raising orchids, it is a large structure made from slats of cypress wood. The slats filter the sunlight, causing it to dapple across the long picnic table that sits square in the middle atop the red brick floor. Used now primarily for outdoor lunches and dinners, there have been three times in recent years where the slat house has been transformed into what Lilly calls "the Chapel of Love."

"We filled it with orchids," she recalls. "There were candles everywhere. We put in all the picnic benches and outdoor chairs. We used the big red Mandarino bowl chandelier. It was bee-u-ti-ful."

Three weddings, two brides (daughter Minnie liked it so much she was married there twice). The first wedding (Minnie I to Rock Leas) was in 1986. Then Lilly's beloved goddaughter Lilly Fowler married Barry van Gerbig on Thanksgiving night in 1996, followed by Minnie II to Kevin McCluskey on February 12, 1999.

Minnie I is best remembered for the walk down the aisle, where Lilly's pit bull, Coquito Rousseau, scampered down under the train of Minnie's dress. Much to everyone's delight, Lilly remembers, "He jumped up, gave Minnie a kiss and then wandered off."

the menu

CUCUMBER-AVOCADO SOUP
WITH CILANTRO

NEW POTATO AND HARICOT VERT
SALAD WITH MUSTARD-
CHIVE DRESSING

POACHED SALMON WITH LEMON-
DILL MAYONNAISE

BERRIES AND CREAM TRIFLE

BAKERY-BOUGHT COOKIES

Lilly Fowler is the daughter of one of Lilly's best friends, so it made perfect sense for Lilly and "Van" Gerbig to be married in the slat house. Lilly was so thrilled for her goddaughter that, when the groom appeared, she couldn't resist some loving encouragement. "Go, Van, go," she stage whispered as he moved into place.

As is her wont, Lilly was walking around barefoot, which prompted Van's grandfather, the legendary film star Douglas Fairbanks Jr., to ask, "Who *is* that woman who is not wearing any shoes?" ("Why should I?" she says with a laugh. "It is my house, right?")

Minnie's wedding to Kevin McCluskey caused Lilly's friend Franci Dixon to tell her, "This is the best wedding I've ever been to. I've never been to a wedding before where you sit in church drinking martinis before the wedding!"

The wedding was also remembered for the six young bridesmaids—Minnie's daughter Lilly Leas, half-sister Jessie Pulitzer, nieces Emma and Charlotte Pulitzer, and cousins Isabel and Maria Donaldson—who walked down the aisle in bright pink Lilly Pulitzer overalls.

The custom of having bridesmaids at a wedding dates from medieval times. Two young girls, often sisters, and dressed alike, preceded the bride in the wedding procession bearing sheaves of wheat, which is a symbol of fertility. Over time, customs changed. Flowers replaced the wheat and the young girls were replaced by women who are contemporaries of the bride—sisters, friends and in-laws to be.

A nice way to express thanks to these women (who, after all, are going to be seen by everyone you know in a dress that you've selected for them) is to revive the lost tradition of hosting a bridesmaids' luncheon—a dress-up, fancy lunch party that the bride throws just for her wedding attendants. It's a way to personally acknowledge each bridesmaid and her contribution to the wedding, and to focus some attention on them, since they'll take a back seat to the bride at every other wedding party. For the bridesmaids, well they can celebrate their induction into the sisterhood of the dyed-to-match-peau-de-soie-pumps.

"Think pink, when you're choosing summer clothes," sang Kay Thompson in *Funny Face*. "Think pink, if you want that quelque chose." Well, this luncheon is definitely the time to think pink. Lilly's

Gifts for the bridesmaid

Small pieces of jewelry. Have silver or gold charms made from the pieces of beach glass you've collected on your early morning walks. (Grace Kelly gave her bridesmaids a gold charm engraved with her and Prince Rainier's initials and the date of their wedding).

Silver picture frames or boxes. Jackie Kennedy's ten bridesmaids received monogrammed silver frames.

Guardian angels. If you're a skilled sewer, make Little Angels from vintage linens or embroidered handkerchiefs. If not, perhaps it's a job for Granny.

Custom favors make your bridesmaids feel extra special. Jennifer Lew made ours, filled with Eleni's cookies fashioned as colorful Lilly totes. For more information, go to www.jenlew designs.com and www.elenis.com.

Best wedding books

Legendary Brides
by Letitia Baldrige

A look at eight of the most celebrated weddings of the past two centuries, seen through the eyes of America's contemporary arbiter of taste and etiquette.

Real Weddings: A Celebration of Personal Style
by Sally Kilbridge and Mallory Samson

Sixteen modern weddings of all styles and sizes are profiled in this delightful book, filled with detailed suggestions and helpful hints. Its creators are the managing editor of *Bride's*, Sally Kilbridge, and noted wedding photographer Mallory Samson.

The Bridesmaids
by Judith Balaban Quine

The intimate and compelling story of Grace Kelly's wedding and the half-dozen friends who walked with her down the aisle as her bridesmaids.

Emily Post's Wedding Etiquette
by Peggy Post

This classic book on wedding etiquette makes a charming gift for any young woman planning her wedding.

Wedding curiosities

According to *Vogue's Book of Etiquette and Good Manners:*

A wedding ring is worn on the third finger of the left hand because of the old superstition that a vein runs from that finger to the heart.

A diamond's sparkle has long been thought to come from the fires of love, hence the stone's popularity as an engagement ring.

June, the traditional bridal month, is named after Juno, the goddess of young people. May, traditionally an unlucky month (marry in May and rue the day), was, in Roman folklore, the month of old men.

bridesmaids' lunch was an O-T-T (over the top) elegant affair. Pink was the color of the day, for in a Lilly themed wedding, only the wedding gown gets to be white.

Make the lunch truly special from the start—an elegant setting with colorful table linens and aromatic pink and white arum lilies—to finish—little pink boxes filled with custom baked cookies in the shape of Lilly handbags for your bridesmaids to take home.

Bridesmaids actually have few duties to perform. They host a shower, assist the bride in any way that they can and are gracious to all the guests at the reception. The one cardinal rule for bridesmaids is that they never—ever—complain about the dress that they've been asked to wear. "How many times have you been told, 'Oh it's so wonderful, you can wear it over and over,'" asks another of Lilly's young friends (who tactfully prefers to remain anonymous), "only to discover that it's covered in blue spangles and cut down to there and up to here and you never want to see it again, let alone wear it?

"Although," she adds, "you wouldn't have to worry about that if it's a Lilly bridesmaid's dress. They are the only ones that you're ever happy to wear again."

Cucumber-avocado soup with cilantro

Serve this refreshing first-course soup in teacups, if desired. Adjust the amount of jalapeño to suit your preference.

6 FIRST-COURSE SERVINGS

1 large English hothouse cucumber or 3 small cucumbers, peeled, coarsely chopped (about 2½ cups)

2 avocados, peeled, coarsely chopped (about 2 cups)

1 medium sweet onion (such as Vidalia), peeled, coarsely chopped (about 1½ cups)

1½ cups water

1 cup loosely packed cilantro leaves

⅓ cup fresh lime juice

½ to 1 whole small jalapeño, seeded, chopped

½ teaspoon ground cumin

½ teaspoon salt

Plain yogurt

Additional cilantro leaves (for garnish)

1 Combine first 9 ingredients in blender; blend until pureed. Thin soup with additional water, if desired. Season to taste with additional salt, if desired. Cover and refrigerate until cold, at least 3 hours and up to 1 day.

2 Ladle scant 1 cup soup into each of 6 shallow bowls or teacups. Top each serving with a dollop of yogurt and float cilantro leaves atop soup as garnish. Serve chilled.

New potato and haricot vert salad with mustard-chive dressing

6 SERVINGS

2 pounds red-skinned new potatoes

½ pound haricots verts or other slender green beans

¼ cup olive oil

¼ cup chopped fresh chives

¼ cup minced shallots

1 tablespoon Dijon mustard

1 tablespoon white wine vinegar

1 tablespoon fresh lemon juice

1 Bring large pot of salted water to boil. Add new potatoes, cover and cook until tender, about 20 minutes. Drain well; rinse with cold water. Cut potatoes into quarters and transfer to large bowl.

2 Bring 1 inch of salted water to boil in same large pot. Add haricots verts, cover and cook until bright green and crisp-tender, about 3 minutes. Drain well; rinse with cold water. Cut haricots verts in half and add to potatoes in bowl.

3 In medium bowl, combine olive oil, chives, shallots, mustard, vinegar and lemon juice. Whisk to blend well. Pour dressing over potatoes and haricots verts in bowl. Toss salad gently to coat. Season to taste with salt and pepper. Cover and refrigerate until chilled, at least 3 hours and up to 1 day. Serve salad chilled.

Poached salmon with lemon-dill mayonnaise

Poach the salmon in two batches if your pot isn't large enough to accommodate all six fillets.

6 SERVINGS

1 cup mayonnaise

2 tablespoons fresh lemon juice

1 tablespoon chopped fresh dill

3 8-ounce bottles clam juice

2 cups dry white wine

6 lemon slices, seeds removed

6 fresh dill sprigs

6 peppercorns

6 6- to 8-ounce salmon fillets (each about 1 inch thick)

6 large lettuce leaves

1 Whisk mayonnaise, lemon juice and 1 tablespoon chopped fresh dill in small bowl to combine. Cover lemon-dill mayonnaise and refrigerate until ready to serve.

2 Combine clam juice, wine, lemon slices, 6 dill sprigs and peppercorns in large pot. Cover and bring to simmer over medium heat; simmer poaching liquid 10 minutes to allow flavors to combine. Reduce heat to medium low. Add salmon fillets to poaching liquid. Cover and cook until salmon is just cooked through, about 9 minutes.

3 Using a slotted spoon, transfer salmon to baking dish. Ladle some of poaching liquid around salmon. Cool, cover and refrigerate, at least 3 hours and up to 1 day.

4 Place 1 large lettuce leaf on each plate. Using slotted spoon, transfer salmon fillets to waxed paper-lined work surface, placing the fillets skin-side-up. Using knife, carefully lift away skin and discard. Turn fillets over and transfer 1 to each lettuce leaf-lined plate. Serve chilled salmon with lemon-dill mayonnaise.

Berries and cream trifle

Begin preparing this recipe the day before you plan to serve it. Use frozen berries in place of fresh when they are out of season; if you do use frozen, choose the freshly frozen berries (not berries in syrup). Thaw and drain frozen berries before using.

6 SERVINGS

½ cup sugar

4 large egg yolks

3 tablespoons cornstarch

1½ cups whole milk

1 teaspoon vanilla extract

½ cup chopped white chocolate or white chocolate chips

1 pound fresh strawberries, hulled, quartered

6 ounces fresh blackberries

6 ounces fresh red raspberries

2 tablespoons Triple Sec

2 tablespoons sugar

1 cup chilled whipping cream

1 cup seedless blackberry jam

1 tablespoon Triple Sec

21 (or more) ladyfingers or champagne biscuits

White chocolate shavings (garnish)

Fresh strawberries (garnish)

Fresh mint sprigs (garnish)

1 Whisk sugar and egg yolks in medium bowl to blend. Sift cornstarch over and whisk well. Place bowl on damp kitchen towel to steady it. Bring milk and vanilla to simmer in heavy medium saucepan. Slowly add hot milk mixture to egg yolk mixture, whisking constantly. Return custard to saucepan. Place saucepan over medium low heat, whisking constantly, until mixture is thick and just begins to boil, about 3 minutes. Remove from heat. Add white chocolate and whisk until completely smooth. Pour custard into large bowl and cool. Cover and refrigerate until completely cold, about 3 hours.

2 Meanwhile, toss berries with 2 tablespoons Triple Sec and 2 tablespoons sugar. Let stand at room temperature.

3 Once custard is completely chilled, use electric mixer to beat whipping cream to stiff peaks. Fold ⅓ of whipped cream into chilled custard. Gently fold remaining whipped cream into custard to make pastry cream.

4 Heat jam and 1 tablespoon Triple Sec in heavy small saucepan over low heat, stirring until smooth.

5 Line bottom of 8- to 10-cup clear trifle bowl with single layer of ladyfingers, tearing to completely cover bottom of bowl. Brush or drizzle with ⅓ of cup jam. Top with ⅓ of pastry cream. Using slotted spoon, spoon half of berries over cream. Top berries with another layer of ladyfingers, ⅓ of cup jam, ⅓ of pastry cream and remaining berries. Top berries with ladyfingers, remaining jam and remaining pastry cream. Cover and chill at least 3 hours and up to overnight.

6 Garnish trifle with white chocolate shavings, fresh berries and mint leaves, if desired. Serve chilled.

PINK

There is a young lady named Lilly

-AND-

Whose dress design proved quite a dilly

GREEN THUMB

She gave it her name

BIRTHDAY

And it brought her great fame

PARTY

If you think that it spoiled her, you're silly.

—ZOË SHIPPEN VARNUM

illy's garden is as lush and wild as a tropical jungle. "I have to landscape with a machete," she says with a grin. When Tennessee Williams wrote about "a lifelong war against the herbaceous border," he could have been talking about Lilly. When you're invited to Lilly's house for a garden party, don't think you're coming over for a quiet game of croquet. There'll be something fun, something lively, something with a lot of vitality.

The rule of thumb at Lilly's is that after your third invitation, you are considered "family" and are welcome, even expected, to attend her outdoor weekend lunch parties. One of the most fun ever was her garden-themed birthday party. Everybody brought something for the garden—all sorts of plants, as well as hoses, rakes, gardening tools, even a purse shaped like a watering can.

The idea behind the party was to be out in the jungle and have fun, not spend all day cooking, so the menu was simple—good food that is easy to make, and plenty of it. Instead of a birthday cake, there was a big platter of bakery-bought cupcakes, each one decorated with a candied flower. Each flower represented one of the plants in the jungle that Lilly has lovingly cultivated for close to twenty years.

When Lilly built her house, she knew what she wanted. Working with landscape architect Edward Durrell Stone Jr., she told him, "I don't want a garden, I want a jungle." To that end, she was careful about situating

the menu

KEY LIME MOJITOS

**GRILLED SHRIMP AND
PINEAPPLE SKEWERS**

**BEER- AND LIME-MARINATED
FLANK STEAK**

**GRILLED CORN WITH
CHIPOTLE CHILI BUTTER**

**BAKERY-BOUGHT
CUPCAKES**

the house properly on the land. "I only had to take out two very large banyan trees to get the house in. I just wanted to squeeze it in without taking too much out. And there's been a lot of planting since then.

"I did not want grass," she declares firmly. "I thought that a lawn would be the most awful thing to keep up, so I put in this postage-stamp–size thing and the rest was this jungle. Now," she adds with a laugh, "the lawn is the easiest thing to take care of and, as for the jungle, you're whacking away at it all day long."

Lilly's green jungle is brightened by a multitude of pink flowering plants. Imagine a pink and green garden—a variation of Vita Sackville-West's famous "white garden" at Sissinghurst. Those two glorious colors. Green means life, earth, bounty, health! It means springtime. And pink!

Pink resonates throughout history, it stands for romance, for hope—"the very *pink* of perfection" comes from the Restoration comedy *She Stoops to Conquer* or "I am the very *pink* of courtesy" from *Romeo and Juliet*. Is it any wonder that pink stands for romance, for flawlessness?

And the two together—perfection!

The variety of plants in these two colors is amazing. In Palm Beach's temperate climate, think ferns; maiden-head, macho, sword—there are endless varieties. Then there are green cro-tons, fan palm trees, arbor cola and crinum lilies. If you're not in the tropics, there are hostas, ornamental grasses, verdant ground

covers and evergreens like boxwood and arborvitae. And the different hues—pale lettuce leaf green, yellowy chartreuse, rich emerald, exotic jade, juicy olive, Persian lime.

From the tender rose pink of flowering Japanese anemones to the sassy hot pink of the towering cleome, there are pinks galore to embrace a garden from early spring through to the end of fall.

If you're in a tropical climate similar to Palm Beach, think hibiscus, pentas, fusca begonias and cattleya orchids. Use the Medinilla magnifica with its pale pink blossoms and dark green foliage. In other locales try old-fashioned garden favorites like peonies, hydrangea, hollyhocks and dahlias. Bougainvillea ("Bougy" as Lilly calls it) and clematis bring a gently untidy naturalness that keeps a garden from looking too "manicured."

For the birthday party, there was a garden plan roughed out—very simple: taller plants in the back, low growing ones in the front, to give the garden "feet" and a nice variety of shapes and sizes in between. But, as Lilly says, "If things get a little mixed up, who cares? A happy accident can be a beautiful thing and Mother Nature tends to know what's best, now doesn't she?"

Everybody came to Lilly's party dressed in their gardening clothes having been firmly instructed, instead of gifts, to bring their two green thumbs and a lot of elbow grease. There were plants, shrubs and a loosely worked out master plan. As people arrived they were promptly put to work planting.

The best garden book

Sackville-West's Garden Book

by Phillipa Nicolson and Vita Sackville-West

Few gardens have acquired such a potent mythology as the one created by the writer Vita Sackville-West and her husband, Harold Nicolson. Their garden, Sissinghurst, is a prime example of romantic gardening at its most successful. Vita's *Garden Book* is a compilation of her weekly newspaper columns and other writings on gardening, arranged by month to take you through all four seasons in the garden. A must!

The best flower catalog

White Flower Farm

Legendary among in-the-know garden lovers, the White Flower Farm offers a superlative catalogue for those who can't get to its headquarters in Connecticut's Litchfield County. Published three times a year, with a witty narrative from the fictitious "Amos Pettingill," White Flower Farm offers more than 1,500 perennials, flower bulbs, annuals, shrubs, vines, roses, gardening tools and gifts for gardeners. For more than sixty years they've been keeping gardeners busy and happy. For more information, go to www.WhiteFlowerFarm.com.

The best tropical garden designer

Denis La Marsh

A former model, Denis La Marsh is the most sought after garden designer and landscaper on the island, though he claims, "I'm just an overgrown kid who likes to play in the dirt." His education in tropical landscaping came from a three-year sojourn living in Lilly's guesthouse and working on her prized tropical jungle. Based in Australia, Denis designs and installs gardens in Palm Beach for four months each summer—"It's the best time for planting and, with the season over, you find the real Palm Beach." Try and find Denis . . . he's that in demand.

Little copper tags were handed out so everyone could sign their name, write a birthday greeting and plant a stake that proudly announced their magnificent horticultural endeavor. The copper tags will eventually verdigris with age and exposure to the elements, turning that lovely green color, fitting in perfectly with the pink and green theme.

Lilly remembers the afternoon with sheer delight. "It was a ball. The kids got to dig and get filthy dirty, so they were in heaven, the men got to tug the big shrubs to and fro, so they felt very manly and productive, and the rest of us got to laugh and relaxed, while creating something beautiful that will last a long time."

The best gardens to visit

IN THE UNITED STATES:

The Society of the Four Arts, Palm Beach
The White House Gardens, The Rose Garden
and its twin, the Jacqueline Kennedy Garden,
Washington, D.C.
The Enchanted Woods, Delaware
The Frick Collection, New York
Chanticleer, Pennsylvania
Filoli Gardens, California

IN EUROPE:

Monet's Garden at Giverney, France
Sissinghurst, England
La Mortella, Italy

Key lime mojitos

Adjust the amount of sugar in this recipe according to your preference.

10 SERVINGS

2½ cups light rum

1¼ cups freshly squeezed lime juice (half of juice from Key limes, if available)

¾ to 1 cup powdered sugar

3¾ cups club soda

10 large sprigs fresh mint (about 4 to 6 leaves each)

Crushed ice

1 Stir rum, lime juice and sugar in large pitcher until sugar is dissolved. Add club soda and stir gently.

2 Divide mint among 10 glasses. Using back of spoon, crush mint sprigs in glasses.

3 Add crushed ice to glasses. Pour mojito mixture over mint and ice, dividing equally among glasses. Serve immediately.

Grilled shrimp and pineapple skewers

Use mango in place of the pineapple, if you like. Soaking the bamboo skewers in water helps to keep them from burning on the grill.

10 SERVINGS

20 12-inch bamboo skewers

1 cup (loosely packed) fresh basil leaves

1 cup orange juice

½ cup vegetable oil

¼ cup chopped fresh ginger

60 large shrimp, peeled, deveined, tails left intact

1 fresh pineapple, peeled, cored, cut into 60 chunks

1 Soak bamboo skewers in pan of water until ready to use.

2 Finely chop basil; set aside half of basil to sprinkle over skewers after grilling. Place remaining half of basil in large bowl. Add orange juice, oil and ginger; whisk well. Add shrimp to marinade and toss to coat. Cover and refrigerate for at least 2 and up to 4 hours.

3 Remove shrimp from marinade and thread onto skewers, alternating with pineapple chunks, for a total of 3 shrimp and 3 pineapple chunks on each skewer.

4 Prepare grill (medium high heat). Grill skewers until shrimp are opaque and brown in spots, turning once, about 3 minutes per side. Sprinkle with reserved basil and serve.

Beer- and lime-marinated flank steak

Skirt steak would also work well with this marinade.

10 SERVINGS

2 cups light Mexican beer (such as Corona)

2 cups (loosely packed) fresh cilantro leaves

1 cup fresh lime juice

1 cup vegetable oil

6 cloves garlic

4 pounds flank steaks

Salt and freshly ground pepper to taste

1 Process beer, cilantro, lime juice, oil and garlic in food processor until ingredients are finely chopped. Place steaks in large resealable plastic bags. Divide marinade between bags. Seal and refrigerate for at least 4 hours and up to 8 hours.

2 Prepare grill (medium high heat). Remove steaks from marinade and place on grill; sprinkle with salt and freshly ground pepper. Grill to desired doneness, turning once, about 6 minutes per side. Transfer to cutting board. Slice steak diagonally across the grain and serve.

Grilled corn with chipotle chili butter

This chipotle chili butter is a pretty salmon color, and it adds smokiness and zip to a summer favorite: corn on the cob. Use from one-half to one whole chipotle chili, depending on how spicy your crowd likes its food. Have guests husk their own corn after it's grilled.

10 SERVINGS

10 ears fresh corn

½ to one whole chipotle chili from can

1 stick (½ cup) unsalted butter

Salt to taste

1 Rinse corn, leaving in husk. Place corn in cooler or large bucket. Cover with cold water and let soak for at least 2 and up to 8 hours.

2 Chop chipotle chili in food processor. Add butter and process, scraping down sides as needed, until chili is finely chopped and incorporated into butter. Season to taste with salt. Place sheet of plastic wrap on work surface. Using rubber spatula, transfer butter to center of plastic wrap. Press into log shape. Enclose in plastic and refrigerate until firm, at least 2 hours. Slice butter, arrange on plate and chill until ready to serve.

3 Prepare grill (medium high heat). Remove corn from water. Grill corn until husks are brown in spots and corn is tender, turning once, about 20 minutes total. Serve corn with chipotle chili butter.

WORTH AVENUE

How much is that Staffordshire

WINDOW

doggie in the window?

SHOPPING

—LILLY

remember my father-in-law, wearing espadrilles, a floral Porthault bathrobe and an eye patch, strolling down Worth Avenue before lunch," Lilly says. "It was what you did in those days. It was no-cost entertaining."

While it might be more advisable to dress with a little less eccentricity these days, a promenade down Palm Beach's fabled shopping street is still "what's done" for a pleasant afternoon diversion. Worth Avenue is, of course, a Palm Beach landmark, but a walk up any city's tony shopping avenue makes for an entertaining—and easy on the pocketbook—afternoon. Savor the variety of luxury goods with a couple of good friends or out-of-town visitors, all without spending a dime!

Worth Avenue was once little more than a dirt road that led down to the Everglades Club, but by the 1920s it had evolved into the city's premier shopping street. Largely the creation of Addison Mizner, its distinctive blend of Mediterranean and Moorish architecture took into particular account the climate and the oppressive heat in the days before air conditioning. The deeply roofed arcades, shaded courtyards and mixture of white stone and red terra-cotta tile balance both an aesthetic quirkiness that has lots of visual charm and a practical sensibility that keeps one cool, so that, unlike mad dogs and Englishmen, shoppers can go out in the noonday sun with no adverse effect at all—except, perhaps, on their pocketbooks.

"Worth Avenue is one of the finest shopping streets in the world," says Lilly's friend Susanna Cutts, who, as public relations and special events manager for Saks Fifth Avenue in Palm Beach, is "à la page" when it comes to luxury venues.

"You have some of the best shops—Tiffany & Co., Gucci, Cartier, Hermès—along with the major designers—Armani, Escada, Valentino and Chanel. You have luxury vendors like Van Cleef & Arpels and all of the Palm Beach–centric stores."

It is the "old Palm Beach" stores that give Worth Avenue its unique charm and differentiate it from other premier shopping venues like New York's Madison Avenue, Beverly Hill's Rodeo Drive and Boston's Newbury Street.

The avenue's reputation for being the center of high fashion comes courtesy of the Everglades Club. In the 1950s and 1960s the club staged weekly luncheon fashion shows—the Wednesday afternoon Tombola—to introduce their members to up-and-coming designers. Bill Blass once remembered:

"I'd go down for a couple of weeks and stay at the Colony Hotel. The younger women were . . . changing the style of Palm Beach."

One of those young women was Lilly Pulitzer. The site of her original shop, at 23 Via Mizner (one of a series of interconnecting courtyards off Worth Avenue), is now home to C.J. Varnum and the perfect place to start an afternoon of window shopping.

"It was fantastic in the old days," says Lilly. "One of my neighbors was a flower shop, and we called it the D.O.A. florist, because everything you bought there died practically before you could get it home."

The Via Mizner was once home to "Lilly of Palm Beach," the D.O.A. florist and a little shop called Au Bon Goût (which had a membership fee of fifty dollars a year to even shop there). "Au Bon Goût used to serve 'flying saucers,' these little crispy tidbits made with cinnamon or herbs," Lilly remembers. Today you'll find Verdura, the Stalk Market, Leta Austin Foster and Arcature Fine Arts.

Adjacent to the Via Mizner is the Via Parigi, home to Stubbs & Wootton, whose annual sales have Palm Beach ladies lining up at 6:00 AM to tussle over their needlepoint slippers. Also on the avenue is Johnnie Brown's, named for Addison Mizner's pet monkey, and chockablock full of decorative porcelains and other home accessories.

A little farther east, wander into Mecox Gardens for their eclectic array of antiques. Stop into Mariko to amuse yourself with some of the best costume jewelry to be found anywhere (go ahead, it's your chance to play Zsa-Zsa). If, like the song, you think "there ain't nothing like the real thing, baby," cross the avenue and visit the sleek Deco home of Greenleaf & Crosby, Florida's oldest jeweler for both the finest in custom design and estate pieces.

Worth Avenue's oldest store is Kassatly's, at 250 Worth Avenue, specializing in fine linens and lingerie. Tucked around the corner in the Via de Lena is Beach Orchids—"the smallest shop in Palm Beach"—that sells, rents and summer boards orchids (pssst, don't tell her secret, but it's also where Lilly gets the fantastic silk orchids she uses throughout her house).

Down toward the Everglades is the Polo Ralph Lauren store, which was once the home of Saks Fifth Avenue. There were apartments above the store and old-time residents recall with bemusement how confused shoppers would get off the elevator and wander around their living rooms searching for better sportswear.

Great shopping streets of the world

Take your out-of-town visitors on a walking tour of your town's au courant shopping boulevard. Worth Avenue is divine, but if Palm Beach is not on your travel itinerary, amble down one of these:

Bond Street in London
Lincoln Road in Miami
Madison Avenue in New York
Maiden Lane in San Francisco
Newbury Street in Boston
The Rialto in Florence
Rodeo Drive in Beverly Hills
Rue du Faubourg Saint-Honoré in Paris
Via Condotti in Rome
Via Montenapoleone in Milan

Five tips for a power shop

1. **Have a strategy,** make a list of your favorite stores and set a time limit
2. **Clothes shopping?** Wear something easy to slip on and off—and the proper undies.
3. **Camera,** take a digital camera with you
4. **Purse,** small and lightweight is best
5. **Shoes,** comfort over style today

Saks is now located across South County Road, in a new shopping center called the Esplanade. Carrying on Worth Avenue's tradition of fine shopping, the Esplanade is home to Georgette Klinger, Louis Vuitton and Sonia Rykiel. Cross the street to pop into Neiman Marcus and then head back toward the Via Mizner.

If you're in town visiting and a glimpse of Palm Beach has whetted your appetite, peek in the windows of Martha A. Gottfried to see what fabulous real estate is on the market.

End your power window shop walk next door at TaBoo, the avenue's oldest restaurant, for some well-deserved R&R. Enjoy an iced tea or, if you prefer some "liquid smoke," try their famous Bloody Mary. Over drinks discuss which of the many treasures you've seen that really calls to you. Then go back and buy just that one thing. After all, you deserve it. Just check with your significant other before picking up something at Martha A. Gottfried's!

A HAZY-CRAZY-

I never repeat gossip,

LAZY POOL

so listen carefully.

PARTY

—SAYING ON A NEEDLEPOINT PILLOW
IN LILLY'S POOL HOUSE

O h how I love those hazy-crazy-lazy days of summer, although you will *never* see me in a bikini, teeny-weeny or otherwise," proclaims Lilly (and, besides, with all those luscious prints around, yellow polka dots are superfluous). "But summertime to me always means one thing—wa wa. In Palm Beach you live in the water. You swim in it, sail in it, ski on it, surf on it and come inside mainly to sleep and get some more sunblock. We live by the pool."

That pool is large and L-shaped and set under a grove of banyans and fan palms. There's a pool house nearby, part of which was the gardener's cottage of the original estate. Stocked with colorful beach towels and pool toys, its banana yellow sitting room has a huge daybed filled with needlework pillows.

Outside, there are numerous chaises, tables, and umbrellas. Lilly's friends are free to drop by and use the pool at their convenience, but often she'll invite a group of friends over for the afternoon to just

sit by the pool, visit and swim. It's a "girlfriend getaway" and makes for perfect casual entertaining.

Why not host your own afternoon of swimming, lounging poolside and catching up on all the news, gossip and summer fun? Celebrate the warm weather with a fruity pool party. Provide the pool, the sunscreen and the towels and have your girlfriends bring their favorite tropical fruit. Stock up on all the latest magazines and tell everyone to bring a couple of old ones that they've read but haven't thrown away, so you can read that story you missed in *Town & Country* or catch up on all the gossipy news in *W.*

the refreshments

MANGO-COCONUT COLADA
WITH GINGER

WATERMELON-STRAWBERRY
LEMONADE

PAPAYA-BANANA-ORANGE SMOOTHIE

FROZEN GRAPES AND CHERRIES

CRAB AND HEARTS OF PALM SALAD
IN AVOCADO HALVES

Keep the food simple: Smoothies made in a blender; a simple, light seafood salad; lots of fruit. Grapes and cherries frozen the night before and served with bowls of sour cream and brown sugar for a decadent treat. If a few too many decadent treats mean it's time for a water workout, break out the neon-colored noodles for some exercise, although Liza Pulitzer confesses, "I'm pathetic. I do a two-minute noodle workout and then call it a day."

To make the party even more of a getaway, create an at-home spa and have an afternoon of pampering and recharging your battery. Yes, you could fly off to Canyon Ranch or LaCosta, but why go to all that bother when you can create the same environment on your own? What is a spa, after all, but a place that makes you relax and say "aaaahhhhh."

Going back to the days of "taking the waters" at Baden-Baden, spas have always been a means of rejuvenation and of renewing the spirit— a nifty way to say "thank you" to your body and spirit for getting you through the day. There are many different spa experiences: meditation, yoga, spiritual retreat, weight loss, holistic treatment and alternative therapies. All you need to do is choose the experiences you'll most enjoy and then . . . enjoy them.

Your manicurist can come to do everyone's nails. Bring a massage therapist over to work out those kinks—there are few things as sumptuous as an open-air massage. Have private yoga lessons or Pilates instruction. Do what you think is fun.

Or . . . don't do anything at all. Just relax. Sit back in the sun or under an umbrella and pick up that old copy of *Vanity Fair* that you never got a chance to read. Then dip into that sparkling water whenever you're feeling toasty.

"Fun girls, the hot sun, a cool pool and some blender drinks," says Lilly. "What more do you need?"

Cool sounds for a hot day

The Beach Boys—Greatest Hits
Frank Sinatra—The Summer Wind
Motown's Greatest Hits
Jimmy Buffett
Caetano Veloso
Ibraim Ferrer—The Buena Vista Social Club
The Mamas and the Papas
Johnny Mathis
Bebel Gilberto

Spa and away

IF YOU'D RATHER GO AWAY TO HAVE THE FULL SPA EXPERIENCE, TRY THESE:

Amangani, Jackson, WY
Arizona Biltmore Resort & Spa, Phoenix, AZ
Bacara Resort & Spa, Santa Barbara, CA
The Breakers, Palm Beach, FL
Canyon Ranch, Lenox, MA
Four Seasons Resort, Hualalai, HI
Grove Park Inn Resort & Spa, Ashville, NC
Post Ranch Inn, Big Sur, CA
Ritz-Carlton, Key Biscayne, FL
The St. Regis Monarch Beach
    Resort & Spa, Dana Point, CA

Mango-coconut colada with ginger

6 SERVINGS

3 mangoes, peeled, coarsely chopped (about 3¾ cups)

1½ cups canned cream of coconut (one 16-ounce can)

¾ cup mango or apricot nectar

3 tablespoons finely chopped candied ginger

3 tablespoons fresh lemon juice

4 to 5 cups ice

1 In blender, blend mangoes, cream of coconut, mango or apricot nectar, ginger and lemon juice until pureed. Add ice cubes and blend until smooth. Pour into wineglasses and serve.

Watermelon-strawberry lemonade

6 SERVINGS

4 cups 1-inch pieces seedless watermelon (about ¼ small watermelon)

1 generous cup strawberries, hulled (about 10 medium strawberries)

2 cups water

½ 12-ounce can lemonade frozen concentrate

1 Combine watermelon, strawberries and 1 cup water in blender and puree. Pour mixture into large pitcher.

2 Add remaining 1 cup water and lemonade concentrate to pitcher. Stir to combine well. Serve over ice.

Papaya-banana-orange smoothie

In areas where tropical fruit is scarce, look for chopped frozen fruit at the grocery store; a few companies package mixtures of freshly frozen fruit specifically for making smoothies.

6 SERVINGS

4 cups chilled freshly squeezed orange juice

4 cups chopped fresh papaya, or frozen

2 medium bananas, peeled

Sugar to taste

1 Combine 2 cups orange juice and all fruit in blender. Blend until mixture is pureed. Pour puree into large pitcher.

2 Add remaining 2 cups orange juice to puree in pitcher and whisk to blend. Pour into wineglasses and serve.

Crab and hearts of palm salad in avocado halves

6 SERVINGS

½ cup mayonnaise

½ cup plain yogurt

2 tablespoons fresh lime juice

¼ teaspoon ground cayenne pepper

1 pound jumbo lump crabmeat, drained

1 14.4-ounce can hearts of palm, drained, chopped into ¼-inch pieces

1 cup chopped green onion

½ cup minced red onion

3 large ripe avocados, halved lengthwise

Additional chopped green onions (garnish)

1 In large bowl, whisk mayonnaise, yogurt, lime juice and cayenne pepper to blend. Add crabmeat, breaking up large pieces with fingers. Add hearts of palm, green onion and red onion. Toss salad to blend well. Season to taste with additional cayenne pepper, if desired. (Can be prepared ahead of time. Cover and chill up to 1 day.)

2 Place 1 avocado half on each of 6 serving plates. Using spoon, mound scant 1 cup salad in and atop each avocado half, allowing some salad to spill out of one side of the avocado half if necessary. Sprinkle with additional green onions and serve.

TEA

If you haven't any charity in your heart,

AND

you have the worst kind of heart trouble.

EMPATHY

—LILLY

Charity might begin at home, but you'll find scant evidence of that in Palm Beach. During the traditional "season"—Christmas to Easter—there are a bounty of luncheons, parties and galas that benefit a variety of charities. "If you accepted every benefit invitation during season," says Minnie McCluskey, "you'd be out three or four times a week."

"Ha!" responds Lilly. "Three or four times a night seems more likely." She adds, "You get asked to lend your name to every charity event, but I really only want to do that if I can actually become involved in the benefit, if I can actually contribute something, and not just have my name on a list."

For many women in Palm Beach, charity work is almost a full-time job—one that these ladies take very seriously. In his book *A Wonderful Time*, society photographer Slim Aarons said, "The Palm Beach ladies have fun, but they also are fantastic money-raisers for local and national charities, having helped to raise many millions of dollars. I often like to remind critics of the Palm Beach lifestyle of this important but often forgotten fact."

The trend for charity benefits nowadays is to go a little less formal, a little less grand. "People want to make sure that their money goes to the charity rather than the party," says Colleen Orrico, Lilly's friend who chairs the Barefoot on the Beach benefit.

You don't have to wait to be invited to help a charity, just find a cause with a lot of local interest—an arts-in-the-schools program or the preservation of a local landmark or the establishment of a community garden—and get started.

the menu

CRANBERRY-ORANGE-
GINGER ALE PUNCH

CREAM CHEESE AND DILL TOASTS
WITH SMOKED SALMON

CURRIED CHICKEN SALAD
ON ENDIVE

GOAT CHEESE TOASTS WITH
FRESH FIGS AND HONEY

CUCUMBER AND RADISH
TEA SANDWICHES

BAKERY-BOUGHT PETIT FOURS

Organizing a benefit is a job in itself and requires a lot of preparation and a lot of help. Ask friends and fellow aficionados to join the benefit committee. One of the biggest steps in planning is making sure people come to the event. How to do that? Build enthusiasm for the charity by hosting a high tea and have a speaker make a presentation to familiarize your committee with the history and needs of your chosen charity. Go through your alumni association to find a classmate who's an author or an expert in a related field. Ask a local architect or historian to talk about an element of your town's history or culture. Most people, you will find, are happy to donate their services for a worthy cause.

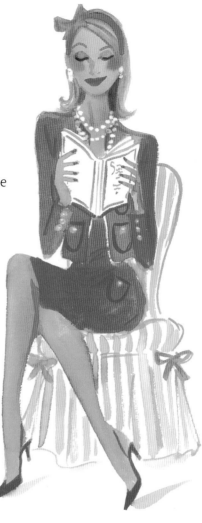

Your tea could be held anywhere, in your home, in the headquarters of the charity or even in a restaurant. In Palm Beach, the Colony Hotel is the perfect venue for a charity committee tea. Built in 1947, it is the quiet grande dame of the Palm Beach luxury hotels. For many years the Colony was the winter residence of the duke and duchess of Windsor. Frank Sinatra, Judy Garland and Presidents George Bush, Bill Clinton and George W. Bush have been among the hotels many pampered guests. In this day and age of casual dress, a high tea is a good excuse to get dressed up, to make your charity tea a real "Lady Mary" day, with afternoon dress, white gloves, pearls, and big hats. It's great fun.

When asked what the three most important elements of running a successful benefit are, Colleen Orrico's answer is quick and emphatic. "Underwriting, underwriting, underwriting. It's imperative, especially in this day and age, to get as many donations, either through funding or 'in kind,' as you can," she

says. In-kind donations means a local printer contributes the invitations, or a bakery provides the petit fours, in exchange for an acknowledgment (and tax write-off).

Next on the list to running a successful event is to ask for volunteers. "The best kind of charity events," says Sue Reilly Diamond, another veteran of the Palm Beach charity whirl, "are the ones where a lot of people have their hands in the making of it. There's a sense of shared ownership, with everyone pitching in."

Third, and perhaps most important, is to make sure you bring your checkbook. "And don't be shy about taking it out," reminds Lilly. "After all, it's for a worthy cause."

Juice up the events

MAKE 'EM FUN

Lilly remembers the Old Bags Luncheon: "It started out as a small thing, with a few women donating an old handbag they wanted to get rid of. I went to the last one; there were six hundred people at The Breakers. Joan Rivers spoke. She was to die for. Funny! Everyone was on the floor laughing. It's grown so much that they are now turning hundreds of people away."

MAKE 'EM EASY

Once in a while, Palm Beach holds a "no ball ball" where, instead of actually having the event, all the subscription money goes to the charity and everyone has a night off.

MAKE 'EM FUN AND EASY

One enterprising charity chairwoman got her local Blockbuster video to donate gift certificates for a rental, then packaged them with a bag of microwave popcorn. Everyone sent in a check and had their own private movie night at home.

The hat's out of the bag!

To top their heads in style, Palm Beach ladies went to Peter Beaton in the old days, but now the best millinery in town can be found at Suzanne Couture in the Via Mizner and Tracey Tooker Hats in the Via Bice off Worth Avenue. If you're feeling particularly "queen for a day," wear a chapeau by Frederick Fox, hatmaker to Queen Elizabeth II since 1969 (and practice that "changing-the-lightbulb" wave!).

Cranberry-orange-ginger ale punch

An ice ring with fresh mint or edible flowers frozen into it would make a pretty addition to the punch bowl. Stir the ingredients together just before serving so that the ginger ale won't lose its fizz.

12 SERVINGS

6 cups chilled cranberry-raspberry juice (100% juice; no sugar added)

6 cups chilled ginger ale

3 cups chilled freshly squeezed orange juice

Ice cubes or ring

1 Stir cranberry-raspberry juice, ginger ale and orange juice in punch bowl to blend. Add ice and serve.

Cream cheese and dill toasts with smoked salmon

12 SERVINGS

24 ½-inch-thick diagonal slices from one French bread baguette

Olive oil

1 8-ounce package cream cheese, room temperature

2 tablespoons chopped fresh dill

8 ounce smoked salmon

1 Preheat oven to 375 degrees. Spread French bread baguette slices out on lined baking sheet. Lightly brush both sides of each bread slice with olive oil. Bake until toasts are golden on both sides, turning once, about 8 minutes total.

2 Stir cream cheese and dill in small bowl to combine. Spread mixture over toasts. Top with smoked salmon and garnish with fresh dill sprig. Serve warm or at room temperature.

Curried chicken salad on endive

2 14.5-ounce cans chicken broth

2 cups water

3 boneless skinless chicken breast halves (about 1¼ pounds)

1 mango or 2 peaches, peeled, pitted, finely chopped (about 1 cup)

½ cup chopped green onion

¼ cup slivered toasted almonds

¾ cup mayonnaise

1 tablespoon fresh lime juice

1 teaspoon curry powder

30 endive leaves (from 5 to 6 large endives)

Additional mayonnaise (optional)

Additional slivered toasted almonds, chopped (optional)

1 Bring chicken broth and 2 cups water to boil in large pot. Add chicken, cover and reduce heat to medium. Simmer chicken until completely cooked through, about 10 minutes. Remove chicken from broth with slotted spoon; transfer to plate to cool. Cool to room temperature, about 20 minutes.

2 Chop chicken into ¼-inch pieces; transfer chopped chicken to medium bowl. Add mango or peaches, green onion and ¼ cup almonds to chicken in bowl.

3 In small bowl, whisk mayonnaise, lime juice and curry powder to blend. Pour dressing over chicken and other ingredients in medium bowl. Toss gently to combine. Cover bowl with plastic wrap and chill until cold, at least 3 hours and up to 1 day.

4 Place whole endive leaves on work surface. Top each with 1 tablespoon chicken salad. Top with chopped slivered almonds, and arrange on serving platter. Serve cold.

Goat cheese toasts with fresh figs and honey

24 ½-inch-thick diagonal slices from one French bread baguette

Olive oil

8 ounces soft fresh goat cheese

4 fresh figs, each cut into 6 slices

¼ cup honey

1 Preheat oven to 375 degrees. Spread French bread baguette slices out on lined baking sheet. Lightly brush both sides of each bread slice with olive oil. Bake until toasts are golden on both sides, turning once, about 8 minutes total.

2 Spread goat cheese over tops of toasts. Top each with 1 slice of fresh fig. Drizzle fig slices with ¼ to ½ teaspoon honey. Serve warm or at room temperature.

Cucumber and radish tea sandwiches

1 stick (½ cup) butter, room temperature

½ cup grated Parmesan cheese

2 tablespoons chopped fresh chives

24 slices cocktail (2½-inch-diameter) pumpernickel bread (from one 1-pound loaf)

½ large seedless cucumber, very thinly sliced

6 radishes, very thinly sliced

1 Using electric mixer, beat butter and Parmesan cheese to blend. Add chives and beat to blend.

2 Place bread on work surface. Spread chive-Parmesan butter over bread slices, using about 1 teaspoon for each. Top half of bread slices with 2 to 3 slices of cucumber and 2 to 3 slices of radish. Top sandwiches with remaining pumpernickel, buttered side down. Slice in half diagonally and serve.

Blue skies, smilin' at me
Nothin' but blue skies do I see

—IRVING BERLIN

True Blue Evenings

KENTUCKY

Mother always had racehorses and her

DERBY

Louis Vuitton luggage was trimmed in

DO

her racing colors of old rose and yellow.

—LILLY

I don't race, but everyone in the family has had horses in the Derby," says Lilly, adding with a wicked grin, "and no one has ever won." The "family" are the Phipps of racing fame and "everyone" means just that: niece Nanki Doubleday (who inherited her grandmother's prized racehorse My Big Boy—a legend on the track), sister Cynthia Phipps, brother Dinny Phipps, mother Lillian Bostwick Phipps, stepfather Ogden Phipps and his mother, the august Mrs. H.C. Phipps.

First run in 1875, the Derby is America's longest-running continually held sporting event. The brainchild of Colonel M. Lewis Clark Jr., its original purpose was to showcase the breeding ability of Kentucky's stables. A century and a quarter later, it's still going strong. The Phippses have had Derby runners going back three generations, from Gladys (Mrs. H.C.) Phipps' Bold Ruler to Odgen's Dapper Dan and Dinny's Successor, racing under his inherited colors of black and cherry.

Though some are tempted to "run *from* the roses," the Kentucky Derby is the ultimate racing event for the horse-loving public. Those three little words—"And they're off"—called out each year on the first Saturday in May focus the racing world's attention on Churchill Downs.

Often called the most exciting two minutes in sports, the "run for the roses" traditionally signals the start of the social calendar not only in Louisville (pronounced LOO-a-vul by those that know), but throughout the South. Preceded by ten days of festivities—balloon races, steamboat races down the Ohio River, picnics and parades—the Derby provides the perfect occasion to have an early spring cocktail party.

Now, you don't have to be anywhere near Churchill Downs to participate in the revels—all you need for a Derby Do are bourbon, biscuits and a big-screen TV on which to watch the race.

the menu

MINT JULEPS

SWEET SPICED PECANS

BAKED BRIE WITH FRESH
MANGO CHUTNEY

HAM BISCUITS

MACADAMIA-COCONUT
DERBY TART

Bourbon means mint juleps. First served by Colonel Clark in 1875, the mint julep is an intoxicating blend of four simple ingredients: crushed ice, sugar syrup, fresh spearmint leaves and 90-proof straight Kentucky bourbon. They are served in silver julep cups that have been stored in the freezer, so that the icy cold liquid creates a shimmering frosted coating on the sides of the cups. On Derby day, "You're awash up to your knees in mint juleps," says Cynthia Phipps, whose horse Saarland is the family's most recent also-ran.

Just as bourbon means mint juleps, biscuits mean ham. "One trick to give a party some juice," Lilly confides, "is to always serve some ham and biscuits. Ham is salty and it will make people thirsty and they

will drink more. If they drink more, they'll have a better time and the party will be a hit." Not that the objective is to get anyone tight, not by any means, but you do want to ensure a convivial atmosphere.

Have the party outside, on the veranda, with the late-afternoon sun and the stirring breeze. An old-fashioned veranda on a big Victorian house is the kind of porch that was used as an outdoor living room around the turn of the last century. Wide enough to provide a deep cover from the blazing summer sun, verandas have ceilings painted a cool sky blue, are furnished with comfortable wicker furniture with big squishy pillows and lend themselves to a relaxed, friendly atmosphere.

Though the setting is relaxed, the Derby's southern roots seem to call for a little bit of formality. Play it up. Put ruby red roses in your silver winner's cup and sprigs of fresh mint in smaller cups. Or fill them with spicy pecans. Find all your old trophies and ribbons and use them as decorations.

Finish the night off with the traditional Derby Pie, a rich confection of chocolate and pecans. The official recipe is as closely guarded as the formula for Coca-Cola, but it's fun to offer a new interpretation of the classic.

Lift up your cup to the winner and, if it's not your horse, remember that you're in very good company indeed (and that there are always the August races in Saratoga).

Mint julep cups

Is a mint julep *really* a mint julep if it is not served in an ice-frosted silver cup? True believers think not. According to Julie Seymour of James II Gallery in New York, "A julep cup is made of either coin silver or sterling, in a simple design. Three-and-a-half to four inches tall, there's no decoration except for a simple beaded or gadrooned edge." Julep cups make treasured birthday or graduation gifts. Each holds nine ounces of what Julie calls "one of the most delightful and insinuating potations that was ever invented."

What to read

Want to contribute meaningful cocktail party chatter? Bone up by reading these three books, one an engrossing insider's history of the Derby, one an acclaimed biography of America's favorite horse of the 1930s and 1940s and one a beloved children's book that was responsible for many a girl's love of all things equestrian.

Kentucky Derby Stories by Jim Bolus "Mr. Kentucky Derby"

Seabiscuit: An American Legend by Laura Hillenbrand

National Velvet by Enid Bagnold

Kentucky Derby don't

If you don't count yourself among the horsey set, don't despair. Just throw a party celebrating something that you do enjoy: the Academy Awards, Queen Elizabeth's official birthday, the summer solstice or Cinco de Mayo. All that's important is to tailor your menu and décor to the festivities at hand. And enjoy!

Mint juleps

Making the mint-infused simple syrup the night before ensures that the syrup will have plenty of fresh mint flavor—and that the cook will have less work on the day of the party. If you find this classic cocktail to be too strong, it can be tamed with club soda per serving.

12 SERVINGS

4 cups sugar

2 cups water

1 ounce (1 bunch) fresh mint leaves

Kentucky bourbon (such as Maker's Mark)

Crushed ice

Additional mint for garnish

1 Stir sugar and 2 cups water in heavy medium saucepan over medium heat until sugar dissolves. Bring to boil, then reduce heat to simmer and allow syrup to simmer gently for 10 minutes. Place 1 ounce fresh mint leaves in large bowl. Pour hot syrup over leaves. Let cool to room temperature, then cover and refrigerate overnight.

2 Using slotted spoon, remove mint leaves from syrup and discard mint. Pour mint syrup into large pitcher. Cover and refrigerate until ready to serve.

3 Set out pitcher of mint syrup, bourbon and crushed ice. Arrange additional mint sprigs in bud vase with water to keep them fresh. Allow guests to assemble cocktails, adjusting measurements to suit their own preferences. In general, fill glasses with crushed ice and add approximately ¼ cup bourbon and 2 tablespoons mint syrup. Then stir to combine. Garnish with mint sprig and serve.

Sweet spiced pecans

Garam masala, one of India's many blends of spices, is available in the spice section of most supermarkets. Hints of coriander, black pepper, cardamom and cinnamon lend the pecans a warm, exotic flavor. These nuts can be made a day or two ahead and stored in an airtight container at room temperature.

MAKES ABOUT 3½ CUPS

¼ cup (½ stick) unsalted butter

½ cup sugar

¼ cup water

1 tablespoon garam masala

½ teaspoon salt

3½ cups (12 ounces) pecan halves

1 Preheat oven to 350 degrees. Melt butter in heavy large skillet over medium heat. Add sugar, ¼ cup water, garam masala and salt; stir until sugar dissolves. Bring mixture to simmer; add nuts and toss until syrup thickly coats pecans, about 5 minutes.

2 Spread pecans out in large glass baking dish. Bake until golden and syrup on nuts is bubbling, stirring occasionally, about 10 to 15 minutes. Cool completely. Serve at room temperature.

Baked Brie with fresh mango chutney

Shop for a round wheel of Brie with a rind on all sides; the rind helps contain the cheese as it softens while baking.

12 SERVINGS

½ cup honey

¼ cup apple cider vinegar

1 large mango, peeled, coarsely chopped

½ sweet onion (such as Vidalia), finely chopped

1 1-inch piece fresh ginger, peeled, minced

¼ cup (loosely packed) cilantro leaves, coarsely chopped

2 8-ounce wheels Brie

1 17.3-ounce package puff pastry sheets, thawed

Water crackers (such as Carr's)

1 Bring honey and vinegar to simmer in heavy medium saucepan. Stir in mango, onion and ginger. Simmer mixture, stirring occasionally, until most of liquid has evaporated and mango chutney bubbles thickly, about 8 minutes. Remove from heat; cool slightly. Stir in cilantro.

2 Preheat oven to 400 degrees. Line baking sheet with foil. Cut rind off top of each wheel of Brie. Spoon mango chutney over tops of Brie, dividing equally. Place 1 sheet of puff pastry over top of each, wrapping ends of pastry under Brie to completely enclose it, pinching edges together; cut off and discard any excess dough. Place Brie, smooth side up, on prepared baking sheet and bake until pastry is slightly puffed and golden brown, about 25 minutes. Serve hot, cutting into wedges and serving atop water crackers.

Ham biscuits

MAKES ABOUT 36

4 cups all-purpose flour

2 tablespoons baking powder

1½ teaspoons salt

¾ cup vegetable shortening

1½ cups whole milk or buttermilk

½ cup mayonnaise

2 tablespoons prepared horseradish

1½ cups (packed) shredded sharp cheddar cheese

1 2-ounce jar diced pimientos (undrained)

½ pound thinly sliced Black Forest ham

1 head Boston or Bibb lettuce, torn into small pieces

1 Preheat oven to 450 degrees. Line large baking sheet with foil. Whisk flour, baking powder and salt in large bowl to combine. Cut in shortening. Gradually add milk, stirring with fork to combine. Transfer mixture to floured surface and gently knead until dough comes together. Roll dough out to ½-inch thickness. Using 1½- to 1¾-inch round cookie cutter, cut biscuits. Gather scraps of dough and reroll to cut additional biscuits. Place biscuits closely together on prepared baking sheet. Bake until puffed and golden, about 10 to 15 minutes. Cool.

2 Whisk mayonnaise and horseradish in small bowl to make horseradish aioli. Stir cheddar cheese and pimientos in another small bowl to make pimiento cheese.

3 Split biscuits open and toast. Generously spread horseradish aioli over top halves of biscuits. Spread pimiento cheese over bottom halves of biscuits. Top pimiento cheese with ham, lettuce and then top halves of biscuits. Serve.

Macadamia-coconut Derby tart

MAKES ONE 11-INCH TART

CRUST:

30 thin chocolate wafer cookies

1 stick (½ cup) unsalted butter, melted

FILLING:

1 stick (½ cup) unsalted butter, melted, cooled

¾ cup sugar

½ cup all-purpose flour

2 large eggs

2 tablespoons bourbon

½ teaspoon salt

¾ cup chopped unsalted macadamia nuts

¾ cup semi-sweet chocolate chips

½ cup (loosely packed) shredded sweetened coconut

1 For crust: Wrap bottom and sides of 11-inch-diameter tart pan in two layers of foil; place on baking sheet. Finely grind chocolate wafer cookies in food processor to make about 1½ cups crumbs. Add crumbs to melted butter; toss with fork until all crumbs are moistened. Transfer moistened crumbs to tart pan; firmly press crumbs into bottom and up sides of pan. Refrigerate 30 minutes.

2 For filling: Preheat oven to 350 degrees. Whisk melted butter, sugar, flour, eggs, bourbon and salt in large bowl until smooth. Fold in nuts, chocolate chips and coconut.

3 Pour filling into center of prepared crust, using rubber spatula to gently spread filling out to edges of crust. Bake tart until golden on top and set in center, about 25 to 30 minutes. Cool at least 30 minutes. Serve tart at room temperature with ice cream, if desired.

PIZZA

You better cut the pizza in four pieces

POW-WOW

Because I'm not hungry enough to eat six.

—YOGI BERRA

The very best of Lilly's parties are the ones that just sort of happen. "Let's have a party," she'll say in the middle of the afternoon, the words practically singing out of her mouth as the idea percolates. "Let's have a pizza par-ty!"

There are few things Lilly enjoys more than having people come to her house for a party. One of those few things is being with her family, so when she can combine the two—her family and a party—she's in hog heaven.

Most of Lilly's grandchildren are close at hand and pop in and out of her house on a regular basis— "Hey, Granny" is the shouted cri de coeur as they walk through her aqua blue front door. Minnie's three— Rodman and Lilly Leas, and young "Bad Jack" McCluskey—live at the north end of Palm Beach, as do Lilly's three step-grandchildren, Adam, Amanda and Christian Boalt. Liza's two boys—Bobby and Chris

Leidy—live just across Lake Worth. "Miss Emma and Miss Charlotte Pulitzer," son Peter and wife Amy's two girls, live all the way across the country in California, so their annual visits are highly anticipated and celebrated with the best kind of Lilly entertainment: simple, casual, sit-around-the-kitch-and-relax, make-pizza-on-the-outdoor-grill dinners.

Pizza has long been a staple of casual entertaining, but pizza made on the outdoor grill with a custom blend of toppings—go ahead, pile on the tomatoes, go wild with the mozzarella—tastes so fresh and so delicious that you'll be tempted to deprogram your local pizza delivery number from your speed dial. If you're planning a family party or having some college friends come for an overnight visit with their kids, pizza is the way to go. It's the easiest way to entertain them and gives you the opportunity to enjoy

their company, rather than spending a lot of time preparing and cooking some big meal. Everyone visits together as they make their own personalized pizzas.

At Lilly's, someone will be dispatched to the local Publix grocery store for some store-bought pizza dough while Lilly does what one of her friends describes as "the old icebox raid," sweeping every possible topping ingredient out of her two flower fabric-covered Sub Zero refrigerators and lining them up on the big island in the middle of her kitchen.

Lilly is a spectacular cook and likes nothing more than to be in the kitchen. You haven't lived until you've tasted her breakfast "granny's special"—a big café au lait cup filled with boiled eggs and bacon and toast "all mushy-mushied up." It is about as close to culinary heaven as one can get.

What's on top?

Are they jimmies? Or are they sprinkles? In the never-ending debate over those little bits of candy that go atop your ice cream, jimmies win (if you go by the dictionary). According to Webster's:

jim-mies \'ji-mēz\ n pl [origin unknown] (ca. 1947): tiny rod-shaped bits of usu. chocolate-flavored candy often sprinkled on ice cream

The games people play?

Board games, like Candyland, Chutes and Ladders, Memory.
Hide-and-Seek
Charades
Balderdash
Duck Duck Goose
Twister
Scavenger Hunt
Card games—Go Fish and Old Maid are two favorites with younger kids.

The best tent

If you feel like making it a sleepover, and the urge to set up camp in the back yard overtakes you, what better way to do it than in a Dre Wapenaar tree tent? The Dutch sculptor has created a canvas-and-steel tent that floats above the ground, hanging from a tree like an upside-down hot air balloon.

But when the kids come over, it's time for pizza and some outdoor fun. And outdoors chez Lilly is very much made for fun.

When she designed her house some twenty years ago, Lilly purposely transformed what was once the botanical garden of a grand oceanfront estate into a jungle play world they called "Lilly-Land." There were swings and climbing ladders, a trampoline, a hammock, a Jacuzzi and even a playhouse.

"The only thing back here when we started was the old slat house and a few remains of a brick trail," she says. "For a while it seemed as if I owned a brickyard. I was hauling bricks in every place. We put a brick floor down in the slat house and then built the barbeque area; that was a very important part to us because our life was the slat house and the picnic table.

"The kids were always in the pool or bouncing on the trampoline," Lilly remembers. "Then there were the mud peeps—the little mud people. When they were very young, Rodman, Emma, Charlotte and Lilly would strip stark naked, cover themselves in mud and then come out of the jungle to entertain us . . . no matter what else was going on. Thank God that game is over."

Should you want to avoid the invasion of the mud peeps, have a bunch of board and card games around to keep the kids entertained. "Twister," says Minnie McCluskey, "has been a staple in our house for the past twelve years."

Make-your-own pizza

Kids will appreciate the chance to make their own choices for a truly individual pizza, as will any picky eater. For an easy pizza crust that tastes homemade, purchase loaves of frozen bread dough (available in the frozen foods section of most supermarkets). Thaw, divide into ⅓- to ½-pound balls, then roll or press out onto lined baking sheets. Bake 10 minutes at 400 degrees, top, and bake another 10 minutes. Other ideas include:

Crusts: Boboli or other prebaked crusts from a local bakery, dough from a pizza parlor, flatbread, naan, bagels, pita or French bread.

Sauces: Prepared pizza sauce (available in jars and single-serving pouches), basil pesto, Alfredo sauce, spaghetti sauce or canned crushed tomatoes.

Cheeses: Smoked Gouda, fresh mozzarella, ricotta, Parmesan or Gorgonzola.

Fresh Veggies: Tomatoes (try yellow and orange varieties), fresh spinach, red onions, grilled or sautéed portobello mushrooms, caramelized white onions, artichoke hearts, hearts of palm or fresh asparagus.

Fruit: Chopped fresh pineapple, mango or thinly sliced pear.

Meats: Pepperoni, smoked sausage, salami, prosciutto, pancetta, roasted shredded chicken or turkey.

Herbs: Chopped fresh basil, garlic, Italian parsley, oregano, sage and thyme.

Ice cream sundaes

There's no limit to the variety of delicious ice cream toppings available, and every kid knows that there's nothing like building your own sundae. Arrange bowls of some of the following toppings on a large kitchen counter (where spilling is okay), and release your charges into their fantasy workshop.

Sauces: Dulce de leche (available at Williams-Sonoma) or other caramel, hot fudge (whisk in mint extract, if you like), Nutella, marshmallow fluff or premium purchased sauces such as those from Godiva.

Fruits: Fresh berries, pineapples, kiwis, mangoes, cherries, bananas and star fruits (also called carambolas).

Nuts: Toasted slivered almonds, pecans, pine nuts, macadamia nuts, Brazil nuts, candied (or honey-roasted) peanuts or cashews, and toasted shredded coconut.

Candy: Crushed Heath bars, M & Ms, Hershey's kisses, mini chocolate chips, cinnamon chips, white chocolate chips, chocolate curls (make with vegetable peeler and large bar of premium chocolate), gummy bears, malted milk balls and diced candied ginger (for the grown-ups).

Cookies: Large bakery-bought or homemade cookies for making ice cream sandwiches (roll sides in nuts or crushed candy bars), plus crushed Oreos and other cookies to use as toppings.

M O V I E S
It's delightful to sit out under

U N D E R
the stars watching the

T H E   S T A R S
Hollywood stars on the screen.

—LILLY

*J*ack used to love watching movies outdoors. He was a great movie fan. He and Jackie both were," Lilly says, remembering her illustrious Palm Beach neighbors. "In the evening, after supper, we would go outside and watch movies on the patio. Not at Joe's house, but the one down the beach that they used when Jack was president."

Lilly had known Jackie Kennedy forever—they had gone to the Chapin School in New York City and Miss Porter's in Farmington, Connecticut, at around the same time. In the early 1950s their marriages brought the two friends to Palm Beach, Lilly as a full-time resident and Jackie as a frequent guest of her in-laws. "Jackie used to come over to the house," Lilly remembers. "She'd drive up in her convertible, with John-John on her lap. She'd sit on the kitchen floor in her white shorts, feeding the baby with a spoon, out of a Gerber's jar."

The two friends would go to the movies at the old Paramount theatre in Palm Beach, an art deco picture palace designed by Joseph Urban. "I loved seeing movies in that big old theatre, especially musicals," remembers Lilly. But after the 1960 election, instead of the friends going to the movies, the movies came to them.

"They put up a large screen at one end of the patio and the projector was set up on the other. Pulled up all around were sofas, lounge chairs, pillows, comfy stuff," Lilly recalls. "Jack preferred Westerns and adventure stories, but, of all things, the movie I remember seeing is *Where the Boys Are.*"

Private screening rooms have long been the luxury of movie moguls and screen divas (in fact, Joe Kennedy, in his role as chairman of RKO Pictures, had the first private screening room on the east coast at his house in Hyannisport). As luxurious as private screening rooms

got the munchies?

CLASSIC MARTINIS

BUTTER PARMESAN POPCORN

CARAMEL-AMARETTO POPCORN

THE CANDY COUNTER

are, they really can't compare with sitting outdoors under the balmy Palm Beach evening sky,

with a soft breeze stirring the palms and millions of stars twinkling above.

Inviting some friends over to watch a film outdoors is a casual, yet elegant

way to entertain.

Since it's after supper, the menu can be simple. All that's needed is

something to munch on—popcorn, of course, and a variety of sweet

treats—and something cold to drink.

With modern technology, there are many options when it

comes to showing a movie: laser projection screens, DVD players,

plasma screens, even an old-fashioned projector.

Now comes the fun part: deciding what movie to watch

as you recline under the stars.

An obvious choice, of course, is *The Palm Beach

Story*, Preston Sturges' 1942 comedy starring Claudette

Colbert, Joel McCrea and Rudy Vallee. It's a zany tale

about the wife of an impoverished engineer who takes off for Palm Beach in the hopes of snaring finan-

cial backing from a reclusive millionaire. A classic screwball comedy, it's jam-packed with delightful ab-

surdities and wonderful performances.

Another idea might be a Lilly film festival. You could start with *Darling Lili*, the musical starring Julie

Andrews as a singing Mata Hari-esque spy during World War I, with Rock Hudson as her lover and songs

by Henry Mancini and Johnny Mercer. Then there's just plain *Lili*, the movie starring Leslie Caron as the

appealing French waif. For a more "art film" taste, there's *Lili Marlene*, Rainer Werner Fassbinder's German

film about the World War II singer made famous by Marlene Dietrich. Last, but not least, *Lilies of the Field* offers Sidney Poitier in his Academy Award–winning role.

Or just watch a "Lilly" movie. What makes a movie a Lilly movie? How about a plucky heroine, a gal who's sassy, capable and confidant. She gets herself into a jam and then gets herself out of it. And she does it in style. Think the Hepburn gals, both Kate and Audrey, think Doris Day, Gwyneth Paltrow and Grace Kelly. Why are these gals Lilly gals? They're individuals, they each have unique personal style and they are all innately charismatic.

What are Lilly's favorite movies? "I love all the Fred Astaire and Ginger Rogers movies. I love *An American in Paris*. Wonderful music, fantastic dancers, sublime."

Some Lilly-gal movies

Stage Door, Bringing Up Baby and
The Philadelphia Story for classic Katharine Hepburn.

Funny Face, Charade and Sabrina for the other
Miss Hepburn, Audrey.

Pillow Talk, That Touch of Mink and
Love Me or Leave Me for vintage Doris Day.

Emma, Shakespeare in Love and
The Talented Mr. Ripley for Gwyneth Paltrow.

High Society, The Swan and Rear Window
(oh, the clothes) for Grace Kelly.

Enjoy the Palm Beach Story? Try another classic
screwball comedy like My Man Godfrey or
The Lady Eve.

More movies

Pick a flick from the
American Film
Institute's multiple
100 best lists (100
Best Movies, 100
Greatest Stars, 100 Best
Comedies and so on).
They can be found at
www.afi.com.
Their top ten list of "greatest
movies of all times"

Citizen Kane

Casablanca

The Godfather

Gone with the Wind

Lawrence of Arabia

The Wizard of Oz

The Graduate

On the Waterfront

Schindler's List

Singing in the Rain

Classic martinis

Garnish with assorted black and green olives (try jalapeño-stuffed green olives for a kick) or add lemon or lime juice to taste and garnish with citrus peel. Allow approximately 1½ oz. (3 tablespoons) gin or vodka for each cocktail.

Ice

4 parts gin or vodka

1 part dry vermouth

Olives

Fill pitcher with ice. Add gin or vodka and vermouth. Stir briskly. Strain into glasses, garnish and serve.

The candy counter

A footed silver dish or cut crystal bowl can elevate any candy to celebrity status. Combine nostalgia with indulgence by including favorite box office treats. Consider the following:

Traditional movie candies such as Red Vines, Goobers, Hot Tamales, Milk Duds, Raisinets, Junior Mints and Kit-Kats

Coconut patties (classic Palm Beach)

Premium dark, milk and white chocolate bars, broken in pieces

Cashew or peanut brittle

Chocolate-covered pretzels or bridge mix

Cracker Jacks

Fruit sorbets served in purchased sugar cones (dip cones in white or semisweet chocolate; drop a lemon drop or other candy into bottom of cone to keep ice cream from dripping through)

Pints or cups of premium ice cream

Caramel-amaretto popcorn

This recipe can be prepared a day ahead and stored in an airtight container.

MAKES ABOUT 24 CUPS

3 3.5-ounce bags microwave popcorn (natural flavor), or 24 cups freshly popped popcorn

1½ sticks (12 tablespoons) unsalted butter

2 cups (packed) light brown sugar

½ cup corn syrup

⅓ cup amaretto

1 teaspoon baking soda

½ teaspoon salt

1 cup (two 2-ounce bags) sliced almonds

1 Pop popcorn in the microwave according to package instructions. Set aside.

2 Preheat oven to 250 degrees. Line 2 heavy large roasting pans with foil. Generously butter foil.

3 Melt 1½ sticks butter in heavy very large pot over low heat. Whisk in brown sugar and corn syrup until sugar is completely melted and smooth. Increase heat to medium and boil, whisking occasionally, until caramel is smooth and syrupy, about 2 minutes. Remove from heat. Add amaretto, baking soda and salt and whisk until smooth, returning to low heat if necessary. Remove from heat. Add popcorn by handfuls to caramel in pot, discarding any unpopped kernels. Add almonds to popcorn and caramel in pot. Toss gently to coat popcorn and almonds. Spread popcorn mixture out in prepared roasting pans.

4 Bake popcorn, stirring often, until evenly coated and caramel doesn't feel sticky, about 40 minutes. Cool completely and serve.

Butter Parmesan popcorn

The old-fashioned powdered Parmesan cheese available on the pasta aisle in grocery stores works well in this recipe; if using a fresher shredded Parmesan, run it through the food processor until pulverized.

MAKES ABOUT 16 CUPS

2 3.5-ounce bags microwave popcorn (natural flavor) or 16 cups freshly popped popcorn

½ stick (4 tablespoons) unsalted butter

½ cup grated Parmesan cheese

Freshly ground black pepper (optional)

1 Pop popcorn in the microwave according to package instructions. Transfer popcorn to large serving bowl, discarding any unpopped kernels.

2 Melt butter. Drizzle over popcorn in bowl. Sprinkle half of cheese over popcorn and toss well. Sprinkle remaining cheese over and toss. Season to taste with freshly ground black pepper, if desired. Serve immediately.

A
In the wickiup by a great bonfire,
TWILIGHT
in the dark green woods, and under the stars.
CAMPFIRE
There's nothing better.

—LILLY

How to best describe a "wickiup?" "It was a wonderful half moon–shaped, half-covered structure out in the woods that was filled with balsam branches," Lilly explains. "And then there were hundreds of red pillows on top of all the balsam, stuffed with pine needles. It smelled so good. We'd lie in there and sing and tell jokes and spooky stories.

"My mother's family had a beautiful camp on Bisby Lake up in the Adirondacks. There was a bunkhouse, a dining house, a gymnasium, the camera shop, the guides cabin, a kitchen and one, two, three, four, maybe five other cabins besides the bunkhouse. There were probably twenty maids' rooms above the laundry house. We had two boathouses and we each had our own tiny little rowboats. I spent the whole summer up there growing up with my sisters and brothers and then later I would bring my kids up there in the summers.

"When my uncle Pete was born up at the lake, the doctors had to row across to get to the camp. There were no roads around Bisby Lake and motorboats weren't allowed.

"Every night," she recalls, "we'd have a picnic. Our guide, Peter Brown by name, would cook. We used to start with a wonderful great fire. Then we'd make reams of toast, bring out this great heavy black griddle and fry up pounds of bacon. Our first course would be these drippy, greasy bacon sandwiches. Then we'd have these three-inch-thick steaks. And *then* we'd have pancakes, followed by marshmallows.

"There would be a big bonfire every night. We'd have a guitar and we would sing," Lilly says, her voice trailing off in happy memory. "As I walked down the streets of La-re-do . . . "

sweet treats

AMAZING HOT CHOCOLATE

IRISH COFFEE

ULTIMATE S'MORES

Lilly has it right: there are few things in life as pleasurable as sitting around a campfire with some good friends. It's a sensory feast, feeling the warm flames bounce off your sun-drenched skin, hearing the crackle and sizzle of burning logs, watching the embers bounce off like tiny shooting

stars, smelling the sweet scent of toasting marshmallows and then tasting their gooey, delicious marriage to chocolate and graham crackers—the classic s'more.

Whether you're listening to the howling coyotes on a mesa in the southwest, being lulled by the gentle surf off the dunes of Southampton or being serenaded by a symphony of crickets up in the Adirondacks, entertaining around a campfire is both easy and elegant. It's the best end to a busy summer's day.

For kids and adults alike, a campfire is hypnotic and mellowing. It takes a party down a notch to a very comfortable place. Everyone's voice gets a little lower and the flow of conversation gets a little easier.

Building a campfire is easy, but it's best always to have in mind that simple question from summer camp: "Fire, friend or foe?" To keep a fire friendly, take into consideration a few basic rules. Always:

• Respect the environment; build a fire where it will not harm the surroundings.

• Make the fire pits large enough to keep a fire from spreading.

• Appoint someone to keep a careful watch on the fire.

• Keep a bucket or two of water (or sand) and a small shovel close at hand.

Once safety concerns are squared away, it's time to think about comfort. Classic Adirondack chairs are a campfire mainstay. It's impossible not to relax while sitting in one; their deep seats, wide armrests and high backs are ergonomically conducive to relaxing. Have a pile of blankets and pillows on hand for those who prefer to lounge on the ground. As you gather round the fire, remember that the night air gets chilly and a stack of sweaters, shawls and wraps will be welcomed as the sun goes down.

The best thing about a campfire is that you don't really have to do anything but sit there and enjoy it. Since it's at night, it's after supper, so there's no need for any fancy menu. Toasting marshmallows and making s'mores is all that's needed. Perhaps offer a savory for those without a sweet tooth and some hot chocolate or cider to drink.

A campfire, with all its associations with summers long ago and sleep-away camp, is a perfect set-ting for sing-a-longs, ghost stories and games. If you have a friend with a flair for the dramatic, hand them a copy of Edgar Allan Poe's short stories, or, if there are a lot of kids, one of R.L. Stine's Goosebumps books. There's nothing like a mesmerizing storyteller weaving a haunted tale as the tongues of flame lap at the night—unless it's a scary prank.

Minnie McCluskey remembers one long ago summers night when "my dad took us out in the woods with our flashlights to the dump where we saw these big black bears feeding on all the garbage. Later that night, while we were sleeping, we heard this growling sound—'grrrr … grrrr'—coming from the dark woods. My brother Peter leapt up, in his underpants, and took this log out of the fire, ready to

protect his two sisters and all his girl cousins. We were all so scared when the bear came out of the woods, but just as it came near us, it rolled over on its back. It was my father, wearing this bearskin rug he'd taken down from the boathouse. He just roared with laughter. We were so scared and Mom and Dad thought it was so funny. And then we all started laughing and laughing."

Sing around the campfire

Be Kind to Your Web-Footed Friends
(to the tune of "Stars and Stripes")

Be kind to your web-footed friends
For that duck may be somebody's mother,
She lives on the edge of a swamp
Where the weather is always damp.

You may think that this is the end,
Well, it is but to prove that you're all liars,
We're going to sing it again,
But only this time we will sing a little higher.

[Repeat the song but sing it a bit higher. Continue on for as many rounds as you can stand!]

You Are My Sunshine

You are my sunshine, my only sunshine.
You make me happy when skies are gray.
You'll never know dear, how much I love you.
Please don't take my sunshine away.

The other night, dear, as I lay sleeping,
I dreamt I held you in my arms.
When I awoke, dear, I was mistaken,
So I hung my head down and cried.

You are my sunshine, my only sunshine.
You make me happy when skies are gray.
You'll never know, dear, how much I love you.
Please don't take my sunshine away.

Other favorites: Oh Susanna, The Lion Sleeps Tonight, I've Been Working on the Railroad

Amazing hot chocolate

The possibilities for personalizing your own hot cocoa recipe are endless. For a Mexican twist, add ground cinnamon; for the kid-pleaser, top each mug with a big marshmallow.

MAKES ABOUT 1¼ CUPS DRY MIX (6 TO 8 SERVINGS)

¾ cup sugar

½ cup unsweetened cocoa powder (such as Ghirardelli)

1½ tablespoons instant espresso coffee powder (optional)

Dash of salt

8 cups (about) hot milk (2% or whole)

Whipped cream (optional)

1 Whisk dry ingredients in medium bowl to blend. Transfer to airtight container.

2 To make hot chocolate, spoon 2 to 3 tablespoons mix in each mug, and fill with hot milk. Stir well. Top with whipped cream, if desired, and serve.

Here are some other ideas for additions that will dress up any mug of hot chocolate.

STIR-INS:

Frangelico

Amaretto

Peppermint schnapps

Irish cream liqueur

Kahlúa

Flavored syrups, such as hazelnut or vanilla

TOPPINGS:

Whipped cream

Marshmallow fluff

Mini marshmallows

Chocolate sprinkles

Mini chocolate chips

Chocolate syrup (drizzle over whipped cream)

Vanilla ice cream

Dark- or white-chocolate shavings

NOTE: Instant espresso coffee (made by Medaglia d'Oro) is available at Italian markets and some supermarkets.

Irish coffee

Consider buying diner-style individual packets of sugar to make it easy for guests to sweeten their coffee to their personal tastes. Transport the coffee in a thermos, pack an unopened pint of cream and bring the whiskey in a flask.

MAKES 6 TO 8 SERVINGS

8 cups strong hot coffee

1½ cups (about) Irish whiskey

⅓ cup (about) sugar

1½ cups (about) heavy cream

Pour scant 1 cup coffee into each mug, leaving some room at top. Stir in whiskey and sugar to taste, using 2 to 3 tablespoons whiskey per mug and 1 to 2 teaspoons sugar per mug. Pour 2 to 3 tablespoons cream atop each Irish coffee and serve immediately.

Ultimate s'mores

This recipe is open to interpretation; rectangular sweet butter cookies would work in place of the round graham cookies, and any favorite chocolate will do.

MAKES 14 (6 TO 8 SERVINGS)

1 14-ounce package biscuits (such as Carr's Sweet Graham Cookies or Wheatola's)

14 ounces (about) premium chocolate (such as Lindt Milk Chocolate with Whole Roasted Almonds or Lindt Excellence White Chocolate with Coconut)

14 large homemade marshmallows or 28 regular marshmallows

1 Place 14 cookies, bottom side up, in single layer on tray. Top cookies with chocolate, dividing equally.

2 Roast marshmallows over fire. Immediately transfer one extra-large marshmallow or two regular marshmallows to top of each chocolate-covered cookie. Cover marshmallow with a second cookie, bottom side down, and serve.

BLUE MOON

If they say the moon is blue,

BEACH

we must believe that it is true.

SUPPER

—LILLY

Once in a blue moon" has come to mean something that happens on a rare occasion—like an evening in Palm Beach without a dinner party somewhere on the island. Dinner parties run the gamut from very formal—black tie and major jewelry (what Lilly calls "hunks of junk")—to très casual—subs on the beach—with every variation between the two.

Palm Beach is fabled for its nightlife, and for all the clubs and restaurants and boîtes, it's the private parties, behind the gates and the walls and the hedges, that offer a real taste of the way the island entertains. Dinner parties can be for four or forty, in honor of visiting dignitaries or just for family, the napkins Porthault or paper, just as long as the food is good and the atmosphere hospitable.

Lilly's dinner parties are famous for their ingenuity, her convivial guests and the tasty cuisine (tasty *and* abundant; there's no need to practice F-H-B—family hold back—at Lilly's). Dinner is served buffet style, most often in the kitchen, and guests are expected, and fully prepared, to pitch in—each person contributing to and enjoying the evening. They are the best kinds of parties—lots of laughing and flirting, music always in the air and often with a Latin beat.

The Latin beat came with the influx of Cubans who came to Palm Beach in the late 1950s. "It started in '59, when they all arrived on our shore," Lilly

RAW OYSTERS

**CHILLED HEARTS OF PALM SOUP
WITH POMEGRANATE SEEDS**

**WATERCRESS AND JICAMA SALAD
WITH CITRUS-DILL VINAIGRETTE**

**FETTUCCINI WITH SAFFRON CREAM
SAUCE AND LOBSTER**

KEY LIME ROLL

says, adding, "not that everyone started speaking Spanish, but you knew they were here." Soon enough, the whole ambiance of Palm Beach was infused with a Cuban sensibility.

In the 1970s, Lilly married a Cuban, the dashing Enrique Rousseau—"You would have loved him. Caca Rousseau, the crazy Cuban." Caca—short for "caca caliente"—was an endearing term of esteem with which he was referred to by just about everyone. "We were very Cuban," Lilly remembers. "We had the entire Cuban nation in our house. The music. The food. The parties. We screamed Cuban, we ate Cuban, we laughed Cuban. There used to be this wonderful Cuban market, La Barata. They'd cook a pork leg for two days—marinate it in garlic and moho. It was so good you couldn't stand it."

To this day, Lilly's house is a hotbed of guests: relatives from near and far, wandering friends and, basically, whoever happens to show up. "I'm one hell of a good cook and I love to cook."

Once in a blue moon

A blue moon means something rare, something a little out of the ordinary. Commonly understood to be the second full moon within a single calendar month, a blue moon appears with a certain serendipity—there will only be three for the rest of the decade (according to the *Maine Farmer's Almanac*, on July 31, 2004, June 30, 2007 and December 31, 2009). Plan accordingly!

Music to dance to

Frank Sinatra is always a good choice. And here's the tip to finding the best Sinatra. Look at the photograph or illustration on the cover of the album or CD. If Old Blue Eyes is wearing a hat, the CD is primo. If he's hatless, you're taking your chances (although, with Sinatra, how bad can your chances be?). Simple rule of thumb: hat = good, no hat = no good.

What to wear

For her, long Lillys are the order of the evening. Dress them up with your good jewelry or perhaps a fresh flower in your hair. Keep a cashmere shawl close by if the night turns cool.

For him, how about vintage Lilly pants paired with a crisp white shirt? In deference to the setting, go barefoot and roll the pants legs up to the "Fred, Fred, the flood's over" above-ankle height that makes no sartorial sense whatsoever unless it's on a beach. Jackets off, but keep nearby in case the weather turns chilly.

Lilly's parties are about fun and good times; sometimes they're themed, for holidays or just for fun (her Cowboys and Indians costume party is still talked about today). Lilly has entertained, and been entertained by, just about everyone in Palm Beach.

"Flo and Earl Smith gave great dinner parties," Lilly remembers. "After dinner we would go outside and just sit on the sea wall; their house was right on the beach. There would be a guitar player. It was all so attractive, sitting out under a full moon, listening to the music.

"Another spectacular hostess was Molly Wilmot. Her parties were splendid . . . the house was very modern and . . . all done in white. Molly would come flaming into the room wearing something colorful. Very gla-*mour*," she says, breaking the word into two very definite syllables.

But for all the grand parties, Lilly speaks with as much gusto about the beach parties up at the north end of the island. There, each of the inland streets share a living room–sized piece of seaside land. Some have little huts and some have wooden steps down to the sand, and the neighbors gather there for impromptu parties and beach suppers. Lilly's daughter Minnie and her family make use of their beach all the time. "We stop by a restaurant and get some takeout, grab a couple of blankets and some music from the house and then we're set for a nice picnic on the beach under the stars."

"Oh," Lilly says, "those parties have a lot of zip."

Chilled hearts of palm soup with pomegranate seeds

If you can't find a pomegranate, garnish the soup with a swirl of cream instead.

¼ cup (½ stick) butter

2 large sweet onions (such as Vidalia), peeled, coarsely chopped

1 cup dry vermouth

8 cups vegetable broth (use canned broth or 8 cups of water and 3 cubes of vegetable bouillon)

1 teaspoon ground ginger

½ cup heavy cream

2 14.4-ounce cans hearts of palm, drained, coarsely chopped

Seeds from one pomegranate (optional)

1 Melt butter in large pot over medium high heat. Add onions and sauté until translucent, tender and beginning to brown, about 10 minutes. Add vermouth and simmer until almost evaporated, about 2 minutes. Stir in broth and ginger, cover and bring to boil. Reduce heat to low and simmer, covered, 5 minutes. Remove from heat and let cool slightly. Stir in cream and cool to room temperature.

2 Working in batches, puree soup with hearts of palm in blender. Transfer to large bowl and stir well. Cover and refrigerate until cold, for at least 3 hours and up to 1 day. Serve chilled, garnishing with pomegranate seeds, if desired.

Watercress and jicama salad with citrus-dill vinaigrette

½ cup orange juice

¼ cup white wine vinegar

1 shallot, peeled, chopped

1 tablespoon lemon juice

1 tablespoon honey

1 tablespoon chopped fresh dill

¼ cup olive oil

1 5-ounce bag spring mix

1 large bunch watercress, tough ends removed

1 large jicama, peeled, cut into matchstick-sized strips

1 Bring orange juice, vinegar, shallot, lemon juice and honey to boil in heavy small saucepan. Reduce heat and simmer until slightly reduced, about 2 minutes. Cool.

2 Pour mixture into blender and puree. Add dill and blend 5 seconds. With blender on, add olive oil in thin stream.

3 Place spring mix in large shallow serving bowl. Top with watercress and jicama strips. Pour half of dressing over and toss to coat. Add more dressing, if desired, or pass remaining dressing separately.

Fettuccini with saffron cream sauce and lobster

8 SERVINGS

2 cups dry white wine

1 teaspoon crushed saffron threads

1½ pounds fettuccini (fresh or dried)

½ cup (1 stick) butter

4 frozen lobster tails, thawed (or fresh, see note)

4 shallots, peeled, minced

2 cups heavy cream

2 tablespoons fresh lemon juice

½ teaspoon salt

⅔ cup chopped fresh chives

Salt and pepper to taste

1. Bring wine to simmer in heavy medium saucepan. Remove from heat. Add saffron. Let stand 15 minutes.

2. Cook pasta in large pot of boiling salted water until just tender. Drain. Return pasta to pot; set aside.

3. Melt butter in heavy large skillet. Add lobster tails and sauté until shells are bright red, about 5 minutes. Cover, reduce heat to low and cook until done, about 5 minutes longer. Using slotted spoon, transfer lobster tails to cutting board. Cut each tail in half lengthwise. Remove meat, and cut crosswise into ½-inch pieces. Do not clean skillet.

4. Return same skillet to medium high heat. Add shallots and sauté until tender, about 5 minutes. Pour wine-saffron mixture into skillet and bring to boil, scraping up any browned bits. Add cream, lemon juice and salt and simmer until sauce thickens slightly, stirring frequently, about 10 minutes. Pour sauce over pasta; place over medium heat. Add lobster and toss until sauce coats pasta and lobster, about 2 minutes. Stir in chives. Season to taste with salt and pepper and serve.

NOTE: If you prefer, use the meat from boiled live lobsters—it will yield more tender results. Using half the butter, sauté the shallots, and add the lobster meat at the very end.

Key lime roll

Key limes are a great Florida tradition. They are smaller than regular limes and more tart. This cake can be made up to two days ahead and stored in the refrigerator, sealed tightly in plastic wrap.

SERVES 10

FOR THE CAKE:

¾ cups sugar

4 eggs, separated

1 teaspoon vanilla

Zest of two key limes

¾ cup cake flour

¾ teaspoon baking powder

½ teaspoon salt

FOR THE GANACHE:

8 ounces good quality white chocolate

1 cup heavy cream

FOR THE LIME SYRUP:

8 limes

1 cup sugar

½ cup water

1 TO MAKE THE CAKE: Heat oven to 375 degrees. Butter 12x17-inch sheetpan with sides. Line bottom with parchment paper that extends 2 inches at each end of pan. Butter paper; flour the entire pan. Wet a dishtowel that is a couple of inches larger than pan, ring it out well and spread on a clean surface.

2 Beat half the sugar and the yolks together with an electric mixer until light, fluffy and thick, about 2 minutes. Beat in vanilla and zest; set aside. In medium bowl, whisk the flour, baking powder and salt. Add the flour mixture to the yolk mixture, and mix until just combined and smooth. In a very clean, dry bowl, whip the remaining sugar with the egg whites until they hold firm peaks.

3 Fold the yolk mixture with ¼ of the white mixture to lighten. Fold the remaining whites lightly into the yolks. Pour into prepared pan, spreading the batter very evenly. Bake about 10 minutes or until a knife inserted into the cake comes out clean and the top is lightly browned.

4 Remove cake from oven and from the edges of the pan with a sharp knife. Immediately turn out of pan onto the wet dishtowel. Quickly peel off the parchment paper. Trim any crispy edges off the cake. Let cool for 5 minutes and roll the warm cake up within the towel. Set aside to cool.

5 TO MAKE THE GANACHE: Make an ice-water bath in a large bowl and set aside in the sink. Finely chop the chocolate in order for it to melt quickly. Transfer to a medium bowl.

6 Bring heavy cream just to a boil, and pour over chopped chocolate. Let sit for 3 minutes. Whisk the mixture together until chocolate is melted and smooth. Place the bowl over ice-water bath, and use a wire whisk to make it thick and fluffy. Whisk in lime zest.

7 Unroll the cake from the dishtowel. Starting at the center of the roll, the tightest point, evenly spread the filling to 1 inch from the far end of the cake, leaving half-inch borders on the sides. Roll as tightly as possible and set on a serving plate, seam side down. Refrigerate until ready to serve.

8 TO MAKE THE LIME SYRUP: Use a sharp knife to cut the skin and pith off limes. Carefully holding the lime, make a slice on either side of the membrane to release each segment. Remove pits and squeeze the membrane to extract any remaining juice.

9 In a small saucepan over medium heat, stir the sugar with ½ cup of water until the sugar dissolves. Add lime segments and juice, remove from heat, cover and allow to cool. Serve a spoonful over each slice of the key lime roll.

Acknowledgments

First thanks go to Lilly. From the start of this project she has been supportive and encouraging. Her generosity is boundless; her enthusiasm, even more so if possible. At one point I found myself standing in her kitchen, pressed into service squeezing lemons into her automatic juicer while wearing a white polo shirt and winding up with more on me than in the bowl—it was a Lilly moment without peer, and I thank her for that.

A quick second thanks go to the folks at Sugartown. Bringing Lilly's clothes back to her loyal public makes them heroes to three generations of women from Palm Beach to Bar Harbor and all points in between. Jim Bradbeer, Scott Beaumont, Kate Kenny, Sandi Davidson and especially Darlene Brinker have been keenly involved from the start, offering motivation, guidance and innumerable suggestions. Messieurs Bradbeer and Beaumont are the proud trustees of a piece of American fashion iconography and they honor it, and Lilly, by bringing it back to life.

Right next to the Sugartown folks, thanks go to—"we few, we happy few"—the team of people who made this book: Nick Wollner, of 1919, who conceived the idea and shepherded us from start to finish, Alison Lew and Renata De Oliveira of Vertigo Design NYC, who not only developed and produced the book, but made the words and images sing; Ben Fink and Izak Zenou, whose photographs and illustrations, respectively, perfectly capture the spirit and style of Lilly.

Special thanks to James Massenburg, Liza Jernow, Laura Meyn, June Choi, Jane Moffitt, John Silbersack and Lauren Cantor.

Extra special thanks go to Lilly's family. Liza Pulitzer and her late partner, Philip Roome, and Minnie and Kevin McCluskey were fantastic help, as were their children Bobby and Chris Leidy, Rodman and Lilly Leas and Jack McClusky. Her step-granddaughter Amanda Boalt was a lovely model riding around on a pink Vespa. Lilly's sister Flo Chase, her brother and sister-in-law Dinny and Andy Phipps and her sister Cynthia Phipps each offered great help.

In Palm Beach we are deeply indebted to all the gals at C. Orrico, starting with Mamma Orrico and her daughters Kathy, Casey and Colleen. Thanks, too, to Casey's husband, Keith Warman, and their sons Jack and Harry, and Colleen's husband, Matthew Cohen a/k/a "Man Orrico." Lua Maxwell and Jan Coniglio worked tirelessly to help us and were joined by Dori Cler, Jackie Gonnella and her children Lucia and Max, Rhianna Jantz, Sara Miller, Sara Norman, Ashley Perry, Karolyn Sjeldstad, Tracy Smith and her son Ben.

More Palm Beach thanks to Ruth Young and the entire staff of the Colony Hotel, Billy Becker, Teresa Moschetta Beresford, Sunny Bippus, Adam Boalt, Jenny Bourne, Katharine Bradley, Pat Burns, Sarah Carrol, Mallory Cheatham, Susanna Cutts, Ann Downey, Jeff Kavanaugh, Putnam Kling, Denis La Marsh, Bob Leidy, Karen List, Cristelle Martin, Jesse Pulitzer, Kathy Ramus, Sue Diamond Riley, William Stewart, Bruce Sutka, Esperanze Ulloa, Lilly and Barry van Gerbig.

On Long Island, a special thanks to Fernando and Marcia Gomes and their children Jennifer and Nicolas. To Monica Gomes, Lucca and Gabriela DeOliveira, Emma and Sage Block, Chris Martin, Whitmores Garden Center and Nursery and the Cupcake Cafe in New York City.

A special word of thanks to Kate Kuhner and her mother, Betty Kuhner, for two generations of gorgeous photography.

Essentially Lilly wouldn't have come into being without the help and support of the following terrific people: Slim Aarons, Catherine Bank, Kathie Berlin, Paula and Bob Cashin, Justine Clay, Howell and Julie Conant, Eloise Cuddeback, Doug and Madelyne Cuddeback, Dick Duane and Bob Thixton, Dominick Dunne, Bob Edelman, Norma Foerderer, Randy Freidburg, Ari Fridkis, Caroline Gervase and Mark West, Mark Gilbertson, Glen Goldfinger, Doris Kearns Goodwin, Charlie Guggenheimer, Laura Jacobs, Josh Kamerman, Marjorie Kaplan, Sally Kilbridge and Bob Payne, Gary Langstaff, Bernd Lembcke, Karen Lewis and Beth Glover, Joel Lilje, Wendy McDermott, David McGoldrick, Amory Millard and Di Manson, Victoria Moran, Katy Mulvaney, Matty Osian, Kate Parker, Charles Passler, Jonathan Pillot, Susan Pollock, Kathrin Seitz, Julie Sogg Seymour, Cindy Shanholt, Charlie Spicer, Jeff Steele, Dek and Kathleen Tillett, Donald Trump, Maura Buckley Wollner, John and Laura Worth, Valerie Zars and all the angels in the room.

Heartfelt thanks to Binny Jolly and Holly Gleason, who know why.

Last, but only because we save the best until then, are the people from HarperCollins. Thanks to Cathy Hemming and her remarkable team; Diane Aronson, Leah Carlson-Stanisic, Karen Lumley, Shelby Meizlik, Megan Newman, Donna Ruvituso, Kate Stark, Jennifer Hirschlag, Cathy Baehler, as well as Stephen Hanselman and Mary Ellen Curley. Let me single out from this outstanding group Kathy Huck, whose enthusiasm, support and help are deeply appreciated.

As always, best love to Meghan Cashin, Colleen Cashin and Kevin Cashin.

—JAY MULVANEY

Recipe Index